GO!

with Microsoft®

Windows 8.1

Update 1

MW01065033

GO!
with Microsoft®
Windows 8.1
Update 1

Shelley Gaskin

PEARSON

Boston   Columbus   Indianapolis   New York   San Francisco   Upper Saddle River
Amsterdam   Cape Town   Dubai   London   Madrid   Milan   Munich   Paris   Montréal   Toronto
Delhi   Mexico City   São Paulo   Sydney   Hong Kong   Seoul   Singapore   Taipei   Tokyo

Vice President, Career Skills: Andrew Gilfillan
Senior Editor: Jenifer Niles
Team Lead, Project Management: Laura Burgess
Project Manager: Jonathan Cheung
Program Manager: Emily Biberger
Development Editor: Ginny Munroe
Editorial Assistant: Melissa Davis
Director of Product Marketing: Maggie Waples
Director of Field Marketing: Leigh Ann Sims
Field Marketing Managers: Brad Forrester & Joanna Sabella
Marketing Coordinator: Susan Osterlitz
Senior Operations Specialist: Maura Zaldivar
Senior Art Director: Diane Ernsberger

Interior and Cover Design: Diane Ernsberger
Cover Photo: © photobar/Fotolia
Associate Director of Design: Blair Brown
Digital Media Editor: Eric Hakanson
Director of Media Development: Taylor Ragan
Media Project Manager, Production: John Cassar
Full-Service Project Management: Lumina Datamatics, Inc.
Composition: Lumina Datamatics, Inc.
Printer/Binder: RR Donnelley Menasha
Cover Printer: Lehigh-Phoenix Color
Text Font: MinionPro

Credits and acknowledgments borrowed from other sources and reproduced, with permission, in this textbook appear on the appropriate page within text. Microsoft and/or its respective suppliers make no representations about the suitability of the information contained in the documents and related graphics published as part of the services for any purpose. All such documents and related graphics are provided "as is" without warranty of any kind.

Microsoft and/or its respective suppliers hereby disclaim all warranties and conditions with regard to this information, including all warranties and conditions of merchantability, whether express, implied or statutory, fitness for a particular purpose, title and non-infringement. In no event shall Microsoft and/or its respective suppliers be liable for any special, indirect or consequential damages or any damages whatsoever resulting from loss of use, data or profits, whether in an action of contract, negligence or other tortious action, arising out of or in connection with the use or performance of information available from the services.

The documents and related graphics contained herein could include technical inaccuracies or typographical errors. Changes are periodically added to the information herein. Microsoft and/or its respective suppliers may make improvements and/or changes in the product(s) and/or the program(s) described herein at any time.

Microsoft® and Windows® are registered trademarks of the Microsoft Corporation in the U.S.A. and other countries. This book is not sponsored or endorsed by or affiliated with the Microsoft Corporation.

Copyright © 2015 by Pearson Education, Inc. as Prentice Hall. All rights reserved. Manufactured in the United States of America. This publication is protected by Copyright, and permission should be obtained from the publisher prior to any prohibited reproduction, storage in a retrieval system, or transmission in any form or by any means, electronic, mechanical, photocopying, recording, or likewise. To obtain permission(s) to use material from this work, please submit a written request to Pearson Education, Inc., Permissions Department, One Lake Street, Upper Saddle River, New Jersey 07458, or you may fax your request to 201-236-3290.

Many of the designations by manufacturers and sellers to distinguish their products are claimed as trademarks. Where those designations appear in this book, and the publisher was aware of a trademark claim, the designations have been printed in initial caps or all caps.

Library of Congress Control Number: 2014941935

10 9 8 7 6 5 4 3 2 1

ISBN 10:   0-13-384115-4
ISBN 13: 978-0-13-384115-2

Table of Contents

About the Author

Shelley Gaskin, Series Editor, is a professor in the Business and Computer Technology Division at Pasadena City College in Pasadena, California. She holds a bachelor's degree in Business Administration from Robert Morris College (Pennsylvania), a master's degree in Business from Northern Illinois University, and a doctorate in Adult and Community Education from Ball State University (Indiana). Before joining Pasadena City College, she spent 12 years in the computer industry, where she was a systems analyst, sales representative, and director of Customer Education with Unisys Corporation. She also worked for Ernst & Young on the development of large systems applications for their clients. She has written and developed training materials for custom systems applications in both the public and private sector, and has also written and edited numerous computer application textbooks.

This book is dedicated to my students, who inspire me every day.

GO! with Windows 8.1 Update 1 Getting Started

GO! with Windows 8.1 Update 1 is the right solution for you and your students in today's fast-moving, mobile environment. The GO! Series content focuses on the real-world job skills students need to succeed in the workforce. They learn Windows 8.1 by working step-by-step through practical job-related projects that put the core functionality of Windows 8.1 in context. And as has always been true of the GO! Series, students learn the important concepts when they need them, and they never get lost in instruction, because the GO! Series uses Microsoft procedural syntax. Students learn how and learn why—at the teachable moment.

What's New

New design reflects the look of Windows 8.1 and Office 2013 and enhances readability.

Enhanced chapter opener now includes a deeper introduction to the A & B instructional projects and more highly-defined chapter Objectives and Learning Outcomes.

New GO! for Job Success Videos relate to the projects in the chapter and cover important career topics such as *Dressing for Success*, *Time Management*, and *Making Ethical Choices*.

New GO! Learn It Online Section at the end of the chapter indicates where various student learning activities can be found, including multiple choice and matching activities.

New Styles for In-Text Boxed Content: Another Way, Notes, More Knowledge, Alerts, and **new *By Touch* instructions** are included in line with the instruction and not in the margins so that the student is more likely to read this information.

New Visual Summary focuses on the four key concepts to remember from each chapter.

New Review and Assessment Guide summarizes the end-of-chapter assessments for a quick overview of the different types and levels of assignments and assessments for each chapter.

New Skills and Procedures Summary Chart (online at the Instructor Resource Center) summarizes all of the shortcuts and commands covered in the chapter.

New End-of-Chapter Key Term Glossary with Definitions for each chapter.

Teach the Course You Want in Less Time

A Microsoft® Office textbook designed for student success!

- **Project-Based** – Students learn by creating projects that they will use in the real world.

- **Microsoft Procedural Syntax** – Steps are written to put students in the right place at the right time.

- **Teachable Moment** – Expository text is woven into the steps—at the moment students need to know it—not chunked together in a block of text that will go unread.

- **Sequential Pagination** – Students have actual page numbers instead of confusing letters and abbreviations.

New Design – Provides a more visually appealing and concise display of important content.

Student Outcomes and Learning Objectives – Objectives are clustered around projects that result in student outcomes.

Simulation Training and Assessment – Give your students the most realistic Office 2013 experience with open, realistic, high-fidelity simulations.

Scenario – Each chapter opens with a job-related scenario that sets the stage for the projects the student will create.

Project Activities – A project summary stated clearly and quickly.

Project Files – Clearly shows students which files are needed for the project and the names they will use to save their documents.

Project Results – Shows students what successful completion looks like.

In-text Features

Another Way, Notes, More Knowledge, Alerts, and By Touch Instructions

Microsoft Procedural Syntax – Steps are written to put the student at the right place at the right time.

Color Coding – Each chapter has two instructional projects, which are less overwhelming for students than one large chapter project. The two projects are differentiated by different colored numbering and headings.

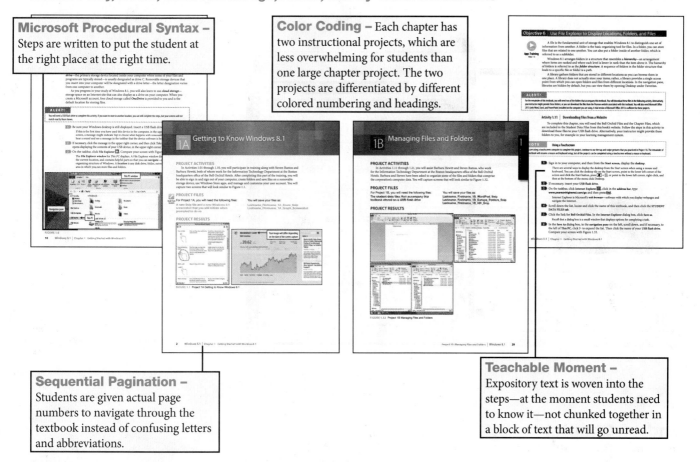

Sequential Pagination – Students are given actual page numbers to navigate through the textbook instead of confusing letters and abbreviations.

Teachable Moment – Expository text is woven into the steps—at the moment students need to know it—not chunked together in a block of text that will go unread.

End-of-Chapter

Content-Based Assessments – Assessments with defined solutions.

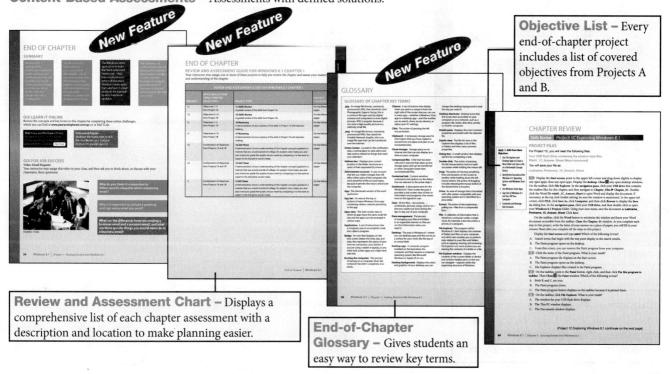

Objective List – Every end-of-chapter project includes a list of covered objectives from Projects A and B.

Review and Assessment Chart – Displays a comprehensive list of each chapter assessment with a description and location to make planning easier.

End-of-Chapter Glossary – Gives students an easy way to review key terms.

End-of-Chapter

Content-Based Assessments – Assessments with defined solutions (continued).

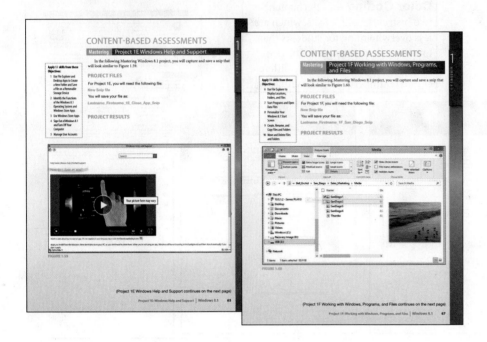

End-of-Chapter

Outcomes-Based Assessments – Assessments with open-ended solutions.

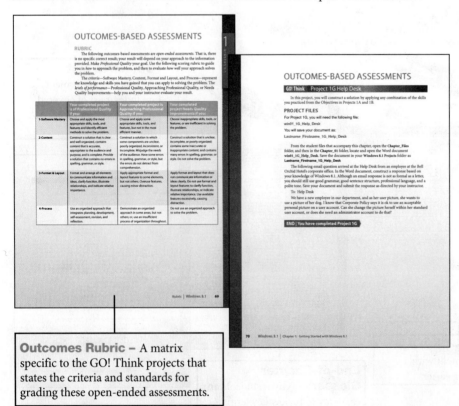

Outcomes Rubric – A matrix specific to the GO! Think projects that states the criteria and standards for grading these open-ended assessments.

Student Materials

Student Data Files – All student data files are available to all on the Companion Website: www.pearsonhighered.com/go.

GO! for Job Success – Videos related to the projects in the chapter cover important career topics such as *Dressing for Success*, *Time Management*, and *Making Ethical Choices*.

Available on the Companion Website using the access code included with your book: pearsonhighered.com/go.

Instructor Materials

All Instructor and Student materials available at pearsonhighered.com/go

Student Assignment Tracker – List all the assignments for the chapter. Just add the course information, due dates, and points. Providing these to students ensures they will know what is due and when.

Scripted Lectures – A script to guide your classroom lecture of each instructional project.

Annotated Solution Files – Coupled with the scorecards, these create a grading and scoring system that makes grading easy and efficient.

PowerPoint Lectures – PowerPoint presentations for each chapter.

Audio PowerPoints – Audio versions of the PowerPoint presentations for each chapter.

Scoring Rubrics – Can be used either by students to check their work or by you as a quick check-off for the items that need to be corrected.

Syllabus Templates – For 8-week, 12-week, and 16-week courses.

Test Bank – Includes a variety of test questions for each chapter.

Companion Website – Online content such as the Online Chapter Review, Glossary, and Student Data Files are all at www.pearsonhighered.com/go.

Reviewers

GO! Focus Group Participants

Kenneth Mayer	Heald College
Carolyn Borne	Louisiana State University
Toribio Matamoros	Miami Dade College
Lynn Keane	University of South Carolina
Terri Hayes	Broward College
Michelle Carter	Paradise Valley Community College

GO! Reviewers

Abul Sheikh	Abraham Baldwin Agricultural College	Diane Santurri	Johnson & Wales
John Percy	Atlantic Cape Community College	Roland Sparks	Johnson & Wales University
Janette Hicks	Binghamton University	Ram Raghuraman	Joliet Junior College
Shannon Ogden	Black River Technical College	Eduardo Suniga	Lansing Community College
Karen May	Blinn College	Kenneth A. Hyatt	Lonestar College - Kingwood
Susan Fry	Boise State University	Glenn Gray	Lonestar College North Harris
Chigurupati Rani	Borough of Manhattan Community College / CUNY	Gene Carbonaro	Long Beach City College
Ellen Glazer	Broward College	Betty Pearman	Los Medanos College
Kate LeGrand	Broward College	Diane Kosharek	Madison College
Mike Puopolo	Bunker Hill Community College	Peter Meggison	Massasoit Community College
Nicole Lytle-Kosola	California State University, San Bernardino	George Gabb	Miami Dade College
Nisheeth Agrawal	Calhoun Community College	Lennie Alice Cooper	Miami Dade College
Pedro Diaz-Gomez	Cameron	Richard Mabjish	Miami Dade College
Linda Friedel	Central Arizona College	Victor Giol	Miami Dade College
Gregg Smith	Central Community College	John Meir	Midlands Technical College
Norm Cregger	Central Michigan University	Greg Pauley	Moberly Area Community College
Lisa LaCaria	Central Piedmont Community College	Catherine Glod	Mohawk Valley Community College
Steve Siedschlag	Chaffey College	Robert Huyck	Mohawk Valley Community College
Terri Helfand	Chaffey College	Kevin Engellant	Montana Western
Susan Mills	Chambersburg	Philip Lee	Nashville State Community College
Mandy Reininger	Chemeketa Community College	Ruth Neal	Navarro College
Connie Crossley	Cincinnati State Technical and Community College	Sharron Jordan	Navarro College
Marjorie Deutsch	City University of New York - Queensborough Community College	Richard Dale	New Mexico State University
		Lori Townsend	Niagara County Community College
Mary Ann Zlotow	College of Dupage	Judson Curry	North Park University
Christine Bohnsak	College of Lake County	Mary Zegarski	Northampton Community College
Gertrude Brier	College of Staten Island	Neal Stenlund	Northern Virginia Community Colege
Sharon Brown	College of The Albemarle	Michael Goeken	Northwest Vista College
Terry Rigsby	Columbia College	Mary Beth Tarver	Northwestern State University
Vicki Brooks	Columbia College	Amy Rutledge	Oakland University
Donald Hames	Delgado Community College	Marcia Braddock	Okefenokee Technical College
Kristen King	Eastern Kentucky University	Richard Stocke	Oklahoma State University - OKC
Kathie Richer	Edmonds Community College	Jane Stam	Onondaga Community College
Gary Smith	Elmhurst College	Mike Michaelson	Palomar College
Wendi Kappersw	Embry-Riddle Aeronautical University	Kungwen (Dave) Chu	Purdue University Calumet
Nancy Woolridge	Fullerton College	Wendy Ford	City University of New York - Queensborough Community College
Abigail Miller	Gateway Community & Technical College		
Deep Ramanayake	Gateway Community & Technical College	Lewis Hall	Riverside City College
Gwen White	Gateway Community & Technical College	Karen Acree	San Juan College
Debbie Glinert	Gloria K School	Tim Ellis	Schoolcraft College
Dana Smith	Golf Academy of America	Dan Combellick	Scottsdale Community College
Mary Locke	Greenville Technical College	Pat Serrano	Scottsdale Community College
Diane Marie Roselli	Harrisburg Area Community College	Rose Hendrickson	Sheridan College
Linda Arnold	Harrisburg Area Community College - Lebanon	Kit Carson	South Georgia College
Daniel Schoedel	Harrisburg Area Community College - York Campus	Rebecca Futch	South Georgia State College
		Brad Hagy	Southern Illinois University Carbondale
Ken Mayer	Heald College	Mimi Spain	Southern Maine Community College
Xiaodong Qiao	Heald College	David Parker	Southern Oregon University
Donna Lamprecht	Hopkinsville Community College	Madeline Baugher	Southwestern Oklahoma State University
Kristen Lancaster	Hopkinsville Community College	Brian Holbert	St. Johns River State College
Johnny Hurley	Iowa Lakes Community College	Bunny Howard	St. Johns River State College
Linda Halverson	Iowa Lakes Community College	Stephanie Cook	State College of Florida
Sarah Kilgo	Isothermal Community College	Sharon Wavle	Tompkins Cortland Community College
Chris DeGeare	Jefferson College	George Fiori	Tri-County Technical College
David McNair	Jefferson College	Steve St. John	Tulsa Community College
		Karen Thessing	University of Central Arkansas
		Richard McMahon	University of Houston-Downtown
		Shohreh Hashemi	University of Houston-Downtown
		Donna Petty	Wallace Community College
		Julia Bell	Walters State Community College
		Ruby Kowaney	West Los Angeles College
		Casey Thompson	Wiregrass Georgia Technical College
		DeAnnia Clements	Wiregrass Georgia Technical College

Windows 8.1

Update 1

Getting Started with Windows 8.1

1

PROJECT 1A

OUTCOMES
Sign in and out of Windows 8.1, identify the features of an operating system, create a folder and save a file, use Windows Store apps, and customize your user account.

OBJECTIVES

1. Use File Explorer and Desktop Apps to Create a New Folder and Save a File on a Removable Storage Device
2. Identify the Functions of the Windows 8.1 Operating System and the Windows Store Apps
3. Use Windows Store Apps
4. Sign Out of Windows 8.1 and Turn Off Your Computer
5. Customize and Manage User Accounts

PROJECT 1B

OUTCOMES
Personalize your Windows 8.1 Start screen, manage files and folders, copy and move files and folders, and use the Recycle Bin.

OBJECTIVES

6. Use File Explorer to Display Locations, Folders, and Files
7. Start Programs and Open Data Files
8. Personalize Your Windows 8.1 Start Screen
9. Create, Rename, and Copy Files and Folders
10. Move and Delete Files and Folders

violetkaipa/Fotolia

In This Chapter

In this chapter, you will use Microsoft Windows 8.1, which is software that manages your computer's hardware, software, and data files. Windows 8.1 also helps you create a personal dashboard to connect you to the things that matter to you. You will use the taskbar and desktop features to get your work done with ease and use Windows Store apps to get your latest personal information and to find information and entertainment. You will sign in to your computer, explore the features of Windows 8.1, create folders and save files, use Windows Store apps, manage multiple windows, sign out of your computer, and examine user accounts.

The projects in this chapter relate to the **Bell Orchid Hotels**, a subsidiary of **Oro Jade Hotels** headquartered in Boston, which own and operate resorts and business-oriented hotels. Resort properties are located in popular destinations, including Honolulu, Orlando, San Diego, and Santa Barbara. The resorts offer deluxe accommodations and a wide array of dining options. Other Bell Orchid hotels are located in major business centers and offer the latest technology in their meeting facilities. Bell Orchid offers extensive educational opportunities for employees. The company plans to open new properties and update existing properties over the next decade.

Getting to Know Windows 8.1

PROJECT ACTIVITIES

In Activities 1.01 through 1.10, you will participate in training along with Steven Ramos and Barbara Hewitt, both of whom work for the Information Technology Department at the Boston headquarters office of the Bell Orchid Hotels. After completing this part of the training, you will be able to sign in and sign out of your computer, create folders and save files on a removable storage device, use Windows Store apps, and manage and customize your user account. You will capture two screens that will look similar to Figure 1.1.

PROJECT FILES

Build from Scratch

For Project 1A, you will need the following files:

A new Snip file and a new Windows 8.1 screenshot that you will initiate when prompted to do so

You will save your files as:

Lastname_Firstname_1A_Zoom_Snip
Lastname_Firstname_1A_Graph_Screenshot

PROJECT RESULTS

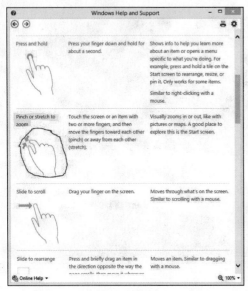

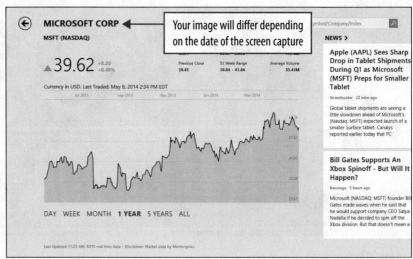

FIGURE 1.1 Project 1A Getting to Know Windows 8.1

Objective 1 | Use File Explorer and Desktop Apps to Create a New Folder and Save a File on a Removable Storage Device

Apps Training
Video 1.1

A *program* is a set of instructions that a computer uses to accomplish a task. A program is also referred to as an *application* or simply as an *app*—the shortened version of the word *application*. Apps help you perform tasks for a specific purpose; for example, to create a document using word processing software, to play a game, to view the latest weather report, or to manage information.

Windows 8.1 is an *operating system* developed by Microsoft Corporation that works with mobile computing devices of all types and also with traditional PCs. An operating system is a specific type of computer program that manages the other programs on a computer, including computer devices such as desktop computers, laptop computers, smartphones, tablet computers, and game consoles. You need an operating system to:

- use apps
- coordinate the use of your computer hardware such as a keyboard, mouse, touchpad, touchscreen, game controller, or printer
- organize data that you store on your computer or access data that you store in other locations

The term *desktop app* commonly refers to a computer program that is installed on the hard drive of your computer and requires a computer operating system like Microsoft Windows or Apple OS to run. The programs in Microsoft Office such as Word and Excel are popular desktop apps. Adobe's Photoshop is a popular desktop app. Desktop apps typically have hundreds of features that take time to learn and use efficiently.

Apps installed on your computer's hard drive are referred to as *desktop apps*. Apps that run from the device software or the browser software on PCs, tablet computers, game consoles, or smartphones are referred to simply as *apps*.

An app is usually a smaller application designed for a single purpose. You might already be familiar with apps that run on an Apple iPhone or an Android phone or a Windows phone; for example, games like Angry Birds and Words with Friends; information apps like The Weather Channel and ESPN ScoreCenter; apps provided by your bank to enable you to conduct transactions on your smartphone; and services like Skype or Google Search.

Similarly, *Windows Store apps* are built for specific purposes; for example, to view your photos, read sports information, play games, organize your list of contacts, or read updates to your social networks like Facebook and Twitter.

ALERT! | **Variations in Screen Organization, Colors, and Functionality Are Common in Windows 8.1**

Individuals and organizations can determine how Windows 8.1 displays; therefore, the colors and the organization of various elements on the screen can vary. Your college or organization may customize Windows 8.1 to display a college picture or logo or to restrict access to certain features. The basic functions and structure of Windows 8.1 are not changed by such variations. You can be confident that the skills you will practice in this textbook apply to Windows 8.1 regardless of available functionality or differences between the figures in the book and your screen.

Activity 1.01 | Understanding User Accounts in Windows 8.1

NOTE | **Comparing Your Screen with the Figures in This Textbook**

Your screen will more closely match the figures shown in this textbook if you set your screen resolution to 1280 × 768. At other resolutions, your screen will closely resemble, but not match, the figures shown. To view your screen's resolution, on the desktop, right-click in a blank area, click *Screen resolution*, and then click the Resolution arrow. To adjust the resolution, move the slider to the desired setting, and then click OK.

On a single computer, Windows 8.1 can have multiple user accounts. You can share a computer with other people in your family or organization and each person can have his or her own information and settings—none of which others can see. Each user on a single computer is referred to as a *local account*.

But what if you have or use more than one computer? Perhaps you have a computer at home and also a laptop computer that you use at school or when traveling. Maybe you have, or are thinking about getting, a tablet computer. The frustration of working on multiple computers is that they do not look the same. Settings and favorite websites that you have on one PC do not automatically appear on other PCs that you use. Additionally, if you get a new PC, you must try to set it up all over again to look like your old PC.

With Windows 8.1, you can create a *Microsoft account*, and then use that account to sign in to *any* Windows 8.1 system. Signing in with a Microsoft account is recommended because you can:

- Download apps from the Windows Store.
- Get your online content—email, social network updates, updated news—automatically displayed in an app when you sign in.
- Sync settings online to make every Windows 8.1 computer you use look and feel the same.

To use a Windows 8.1 computer, you must establish and then sign in with either a local account or a Microsoft account. Regardless of which one you select, you should provide an email address to associate with the user account name.

If you create and then sign in with a local account, you can still connect to the Internet, but you will not have the advantage of having your personal arrangement of apps displayed to you every time you sign in to a Windows 8.1 PC. As shown in Figure 1.2, a new user added to a Windows 8.1 PC can provide an email address to associate with the account. You can use any email address to create a local account—similar to other online services where an email address is your user ID.

FIGURE 1.2

To create a Microsoft account, supply a **hotmail.com**, a **live.com**, an **msn.com**, or an **outlook.com** email address—or create a new free Microsoft account from the link *Sign up for a new email address* to display the form for a new Microsoft account. After you create a Microsoft account, you *do not* have to use it for your email or for any purpose other than to use the Windows 8.1 interface and to *roam* all of your computing devices. To roam means that you can set up one computer, for example your desktop computer, and then synchronize—roam—all the same settings to your laptop, to your tablet PC, to your Windows phone—to any other device you have that uses Windows 8.1.

By signing in with a Microsoft account, your computer becomes your connected device where you—not your files—are the center of activity.

To check how well you understand user accounts in Windows 8.1, take a moment to answer the following questions:

1 ▸ On a single Windows 8.1 computer, multiple people can have a user account with their own information and _____.

2 ▸ On a Windows 8.1 computer, it is recommended that you create a Microsoft account—if you do not have one—and then use that account to sign in because you can sync settings online to make every Windows 8.1 computer you sign in to _____ and feel the same.

3 ▸ To use a Windows 8.1 computer, you must establish and then sign in with either a _____ account or a Microsoft account.

4 ▸ After you create a Microsoft account, you do not have to use it for your _____ or for any other purpose.

5 ▸ To _____ means that you can set up one computer and then sync (synchronize) all the same settings to any other device you have that uses Windows 8.1.

Activity 1.02 | **Turning On Your Computer, Signing In to a Windows 8.1 User Account, and Exploring the Windows 8.1 Environment**

Before you begin any computer activity, you must, if necessary, turn on your computer. This process is commonly referred to as *booting the computer*. Because Windows 8.1 does not require you to completely shut down your computer except to install or repair a hardware device, in most instances moving the mouse or pressing a key will wake your computer in a few seconds. So most of the time you will skip the lengthier boot process.

In this activity, you will turn on your computer and sign in to Windows 8.1. Within an organization, the sign-in process may differ from that of your own computer.

ALERT! | **You must have a user account—preferably a Microsoft account—on the computer at which you are working.**

On a Windows 8.1 PC, you must have a user account in order to sign in. On your own computer, you created your user account when you installed Windows 8.1 or when you set up your new computer that came with Windows 8.1. In a classroom or lab, check with your instructor to see how you will sign in to Windows 8.1. Recall that signing in with a Microsoft account, as described in the previous activity, will enable you to use apps with updated data.

---

1 ▸ If necessary, turn on your computer, and then compare your screen with Figure 1.3.

The Windows 8.1 *lock screen* displays a picture—this might be a default picture, or a picture that you selected if you have personalized your system already. You can also choose to have a slide show of your own photos display on the lock screen.

The lock screen displays the time, day, and date, and one or more icons—sometimes referred to as *badges*—representing the status of your Internet connection, your battery if you are using a tablet or laptop, and any *lock screen apps* you might have selected. A lock screen app runs in the background and shows you quick status and notifications, even when your screen is locked.

For example, one lock screen app that you can add is Skype, so that you can answer a Skype call without having to sign in.

Your organization might have a custom sign-in screen with a logo or sign-in instructions, which will differ from the one shown.

Lock screen picture
(yours may differ)

12:10

Time/Day/Date
(yours will differ)

Monday, November 18

Icons can display under date indicating Internet connection
status, battery status, and other indicators (none shown here)

FIGURE 1.3

2 Determine whether you are working with a mouse and keyboard system or with a touchscreen system. If you are working with a touchscreen, determine whether you will use a stylus pen or the touch of your fingers.

Windows 8.1 is optimized for touchscreen computers and also works with a mouse and keyboard in the way you are probably most accustomed. If your device has a touchscreen, you can use the following gestures with your fingers in place of mouse and keyboard commands:

- Tap an item to click it.
- Press and hold an item for a few seconds and then release to right-click it.
- Touch the screen or an item with two or more fingers and then pinch together to zoom in or stretch your fingers apart to zoom out.
- Slide to scroll—drag your finger on the screen to move through what's on the screen; similar to scrolling with a mouse.
- Slide to rearrange—similar to dragging with a mouse.
- Swipe to select—slide an item a short distance with a quick movement to select an item and bring up app commands, if any.
- Swipe from edge—from right to open charms; from left to view or switch among open apps or close apps; from top or bottom to show commands or close an app.

NOTE   **This Book Assumes You Are Using a Mouse and Keyboard, but You Can Also Use Touch**

The instruction in this textbook uses terminology that assumes you are using a mouse and keyboard, but you need only substitute the gestures listed above to move through the instruction easily using touch. If a touch gesture needs more clarification, a *By Touch* box will assist you in using the correct gesture. Because more precision is needed for desktop operations, touching with a stylus pen may be preferable to touch using your fingers. When working with Windows Store apps, finger gestures are precise.

3 Press [Enter] to display the Windows 8.1 sign-in screen.

 BY TOUCH   On the lock screen, swipe upward to display the sign-in screen. Tap your user image if necessary to display the Password box.

4 If you are the displayed user, type your password (if you have established one) and press Enter. If you are not the displayed user, click your user image if it displays or click the **Switch user arrow** ⊙ and then click your user image. Type your password, and then compare your screen with Figure 1.4.

ALERT!

PCs that do not have a touchscreen are set to default to the desktop instead of the Start screen. If you do not see the Start screen, in the lower left corner of your screen, click the Start button ⊞.

The Windows 8.1 *Start screen* displays with square and rectangular boxes—referred to as *tiles*—from which you can access apps, websites, programs, and tools for using your computer by simply clicking or tapping them.

Think of the Start screen as your connected *dashboard*—a one-screen view of links to information and programs that matter to *you*—through which you can connect with the people, activities, places, and apps that you care about. Some tiles are referred to as *live tiles*, meaning they are constantly updated with fresh information relevant to you—the number of new email messages you have, new sports scores that you are interested in, or new updates to social networks such as Facebook or Twitter. Live tiles are at the center of your Windows 8.1 experience.

As you progress in your study of Windows 8.1, you will learn to customize the Start screen and add, delete, and organize tiles into meaningful groups. Your Start screen will not look like anyone else's; you will customize it to suit your own information needs.

FIGURE 1.4

NOTE   **Differing Sign-In Procedures and Passwords**

Depending on whether you are working on your own computer, in a college lab, or in an organization, your sign-in process may differ. If you have a different sign-in screen, sign in as directed and move to Step 5 of this activity. If you are working in a classroom or lab, ask your instructor or lab assistant about the user account name and password to use. On your own computer, use your own user account name and password if you established a password.

5 > On your **Start screen**, locate and then move the mouse pointer over—*point to*—the **Desktop tile**, and then *click*—press the left button on your mouse pointing device—to display the **Windows desktop**.

The *mouse pointer* is any symbol that displays on your screen in response to moving your mouse.

⟳ BY TOUCH   Tap the Windows desktop tile.

6 > Compare your screen with Figure 1.5, and then take a moment to study the parts of the Windows desktop as shown in the table in Figure 1.6.

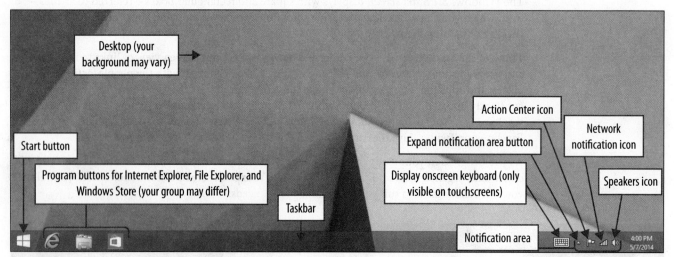

FIGURE 1.5

FIGURE 1.6

PARTS OF THE WINDOWS 8.1 DESKTOP	
Action Center icon in the notification area	Displays the **Action Center**—a central place to view alerts and take actions related to things that need your attention.
Desktop	Serves as a surface for your work, like the top of an actual desk. Here you can arrange *icons*—small pictures that represent a file, folder, program, or other object.
Desktop background	Displays the colors and graphics of your desktop; you can change the *desktop background* to look the way you want it, such as using a picture or a solid color. Also referred to as *wallpaper*.
Expand notification area button	Displays additional icons related to your notifications.
Network notification icon	Displays the status of your network.
Notification area	Displays notification icons and the system clock and calendar; sometimes referred to as the *system tray*.
Start button	Displays the Start screen.
Program buttons	Launch **Internet Explorer**, Microsoft's web browser that is included with Windows 8.1, **File Explorer**, the program that displays locations, folders, and files on your computer, and also enables you to perform tasks related to your files and folders such as copying, moving, and renaming, and Windows Store to find apps.
Recycle Bin	Contains files and folders that you delete. When you delete a file or folder, it is not actually deleted; it stays in the Recycle Bin if you want it back, until you take an action to empty the Recycle Bin.
Speakers icon	Displays the status of your computer's speakers (if any).
Taskbar	Contains the Start button, program buttons to launch programs, and buttons for all open programs; by default, it is located at the bottom of the desktop, but you can move it. You can customize the number and arrangement of buttons.

Activity 1.03 | Pinning a Program to the Taskbar

Snipping Tool is a program within Windows that captures an image of all or part of your computer's screen within desktop apps. A ***snip***, as the captured image is called, can be annotated, saved, copied, or shared via email. This is also referred to as a ***screen capture*** or a ***screenshot***.

1 In the lower left corner of your screen, click the **Start** button ⊞ one time to display the **Start screen**. Although you will not immediately see your typing, begin to type **snipping** and then compare your screen with Figure 1.7.

> From the desktop, the easiest and fastest way to search for an app is to display the Start screen and begin to type. By default, Windows 8.1 searches *Everywhere*, but you can narrow the search to Settings, Files, Web images, and Web videos. The built-in functionality of ***Bing Smart Search*** searches your PC, the web, and OneDrive, plus some apps and the Windows store. And, you can go back to your search results and without having to search again.

 BY TOUCH On a touchscreen, swipe in from right edge of the screen, and then tap Search. Tap in the Search box to display the onscreen keyboard, and then begin to type *snipping*.

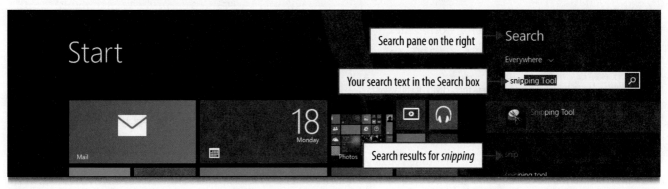

FIGURE 1.7

2 With **Snipping Tool** selected—shaded, referred to as the *focus* of the search—press ⏎ one time.

> The desktop redisplays, the Snipping Tool ***dialog box*** displays on the desktop, and on the taskbar, the Snipping Tool program button displays framed in a lighter shade to indicate that the program is open.
>
> A dialog box is a small window that displays options for completing a task.

 BY TOUCH In the search results, tap the Snipping Tool app.

3 On the taskbar, point to the **Snipping Tool program button** 📷 and then ***right-click***—click the right mouse button one time. On the displayed **Jump List**, click **Pin this program to taskbar**.

> A ***Jump List*** displays destinations and tasks from a program's taskbar button.

 BY TOUCH On the taskbar, use the *Swipe to select* technique—swipe upward with a short quick movement—to display the Jump List. On the list, tap *Pin this program to taskbar*.

4 Point to the upper right corner of the **Snipping Tool** dialog box, and then click **Close** ⊠.

> Because you will use Snipping Tool frequently while completing the projects in this instruction, it is recommended that you leave Snipping Tool pinned to your taskbar.

Activity 1.04 | Creating a New Folder on a Removable Storage Device

A *file* is a collection of information stored on a computer under a single name. Examples of a file include a Word document, an Excel workbook, a picture, a song, or a program. A *folder* is a container in which you can store files. Windows 8.1 organizes and keeps track of your electronic files by letting you create and label electronic folders into which you can place your files.

In this activity, you will create a new folder on a *removable storage device*. Removable storage devices, such as a USB flash drive, are commonly used to transfer information from one computer to another. Such devices are also useful when you want to work with your files on different computers. For example, you probably have files that you work with at your college, at home, and possibly at your workplace.

A *drive* is an area of storage that is formatted with a file system compatible with your operating system and is identified by a drive letter. For example, your computer's *hard disk drive*—the primary storage device located inside your computer where some of your files and programs are typically stored—is usually designated as drive C. Removable storage devices that you insert into your computer will be designated with a drive letter—the letter designation varies from one computer to another.

As you progress in your study of Windows 8.1, you will also learn to use *cloud storage*—storage space on an Internet site that can also display as a drive on your computer. When you create a Microsoft account, free cloud storage called *OneDrive* is provided to you and is the default location for storing files.

> **ALERT!**
>
> You will need a USB flash drive to complete this activity. If you want to store in another location, you can still complete the steps, but your screens will not match exactly those shown.

1 ▶ Be sure your Windows desktop is still displayed. Insert a USB flash drive into your computer.

If this is the first time you have used this device in the computer, in the upper right portion of your screen, a message might indicate *Tap to choose what happens with removable drives*. You might also hear a sound and see a message in the taskbar that the device software is being installed.

2 ▶ If necessary, click the message in the upper right corner, and then click *Take no action*. If a window opens displaying the contents of your USB device, in the upper right corner click **Close** ☒.

3 ▶ On the taskbar, click **File Explorer** 🗔. Compare your screen with Figure 1.8.

The *File Explorer window* for *This PC* displays. A File Explorer window displays the contents of the current location, and contains helpful parts so that you can *navigate*—explore within the file organizing structure of Windows. A *location* is any disk drive, folder, network, or cloud storage area in which you can store files and folders.

FIGURE 1.8

4 If necessary, in the upper right corner of the **This PC** window, click **Expand the Ribbon** ⌄ and then compare your screen with Figure 1.9.

Use the *navigation pane*—the area on the left side of File Explorer window—to get to locations—your OneDrive, folders on your PC, devices and drives connected to your PC, and other PCs on your network.

The *ribbon* is a user interface in Windows 8.1 that groups commands for performing related tasks on tabs across the upper portion of a window. Commands for common tasks include copying and moving, creating new folders, emailing and zipping items, and changing the view.

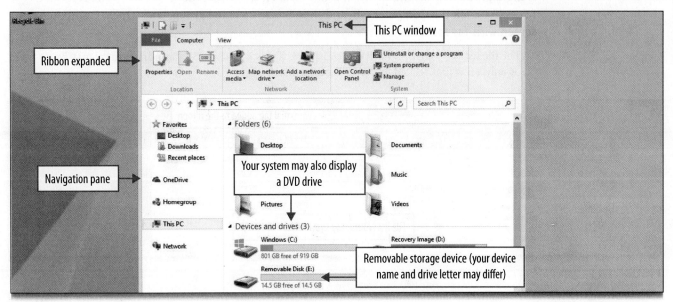

FIGURE 1.9

5 Under **Devices and drives**, locate **Windows (C:)**—or OS (C:) or Local disk (C:)—point to the device name to display the ▯ pointer, and then right-click to display a shortcut menu. Compare your screen with Figure 1.10.

A *shortcut menu* is a context-sensitive menu that displays commands and options relevant to the active object.

BY TOUCH Press and hold briefly to display a shaded square and then release.

FIGURE 1.10

6 On the shortcut menu, click **Open** to display the *file list* for this drive.

A file list displays the contents of the current folder or location. If you enter a search term in the search box, you results will also display in the file list. Here, in the C: drive, Windows 8.1 stores various files related to your operating system. The Windows logo on the C: drive indicates this is where the Windows 8.1 operating system is stored.

ANOTHER WAY Point to the device name and double-click to display the file list for the device.

7 To the left of the **address bar**, click the **Up** button ⬆ to move up one level in the drive hierarchy and close the file list.

The *address bar* displays your current location in the folder structure as a series of links separated by arrows. Use the address bar to enter or select a location. You can tap or click a part of the series of links to go to that level, or tap or click at the end of the series of links to select the path for copying.

8 Under **Devices and drives**, click your **USB flash drive** to select it, and notice that the drive is highlighted in blue, indicating it is selected. At the top of the window, on the ribbon, if necessary click the **Computer tab**, and then in the **Location group**, click **Open**. Compare your screen with Figure 1.11.

The file list for your USB flash drive displays. If this is a new USB flash drive, there may be no files or only a few files related to the USB device itself.

FIGURE 1.11

NOTE **Does your ribbon show only the tab names?**

By default, the ribbon is minimized and appears as a menu bar, displaying only the ribbon tabs. If only the tabs of your ribbon are displayed, click the Expand the Ribbon arrow ⌄ on the right side to display the full ribbon.

---

9 On the ribbon, notice that **Drive Tools** displays above the **Manage tab**.

This is a *contextual tab*, which is a tab added to the ribbon when a specific object is selected and that contains commands relevant to the selected object.

10 On the ribbon, in the **New group**, click **New folder**.

11 With the text *New folder* highlighted in blue, type **Windows 8.1 Projects** and press Enter to confirm the folder name and select—highlight in blue—the new folder. With the folder selected, press Enter again to open the File Explorer window for your **Windows 8.1 Projects** folder. Compare your screen with Figure 1.12.

To *select* means to specify, by highlighting, a block of data or text on the screen with the intent of performing some action on the selection.

A new folder is created on your removable storage device. The address bar indicates the *path* from This PC to your device and then to your folder. A path is a sequence of folders that leads to a specific file or folder.

↻ **BY TOUCH**   You may have to tap the keyboard icon in the lower right corner of the taskbar to display the onscreen keyboard.

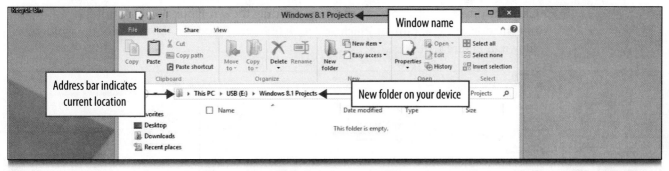

FIGURE 1.12

Activity 1.05 | Creating and Saving a File

1 In the upper right corner of the window, click **Help** 🔲, and then under the **Search** box, click **Help home**. Click **Get started**, and then click **Touch: swipe, tap, and beyond**. Compare your screen with Figure 1.13.

A vertical *scroll bar* displays on the right side of this window. A scroll bar displays when the contents of a window are not completely visible. A scroll bar can be vertical as shown or horizontal and displayed at the bottom of a window.

Within the scroll bar, you can move the *scroll box* to bring the contents of the window into view. The position of the scroll box within the scroll bar indicates your relative position within the window's contents. You can click the *scroll arrow* at either end of the scroll bar to move within the window in small increments.

Each computer manufacturer has some control over the Windows Help and Support opening screen. At the top of this screen, the manufacturer may place links to its own support and information about your computer's hardware.

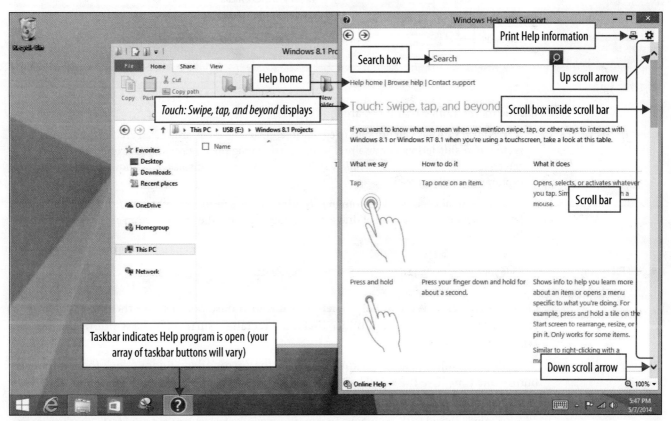

FIGURE 1.13

2 Click the down scroll arrow as necessary—or drag the scroll box down—until the information and diagram for **Pinch or stretch to zoom** displays in the center of the window, as shown in Figure 1.14.

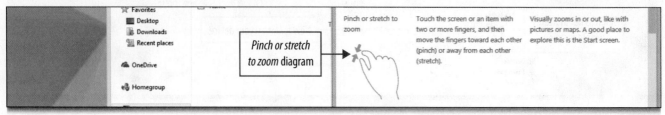

FIGURE 1.14

3 On the taskbar, click the **Snipping Tool** button to display the small **Snipping Tool** window.

4 On the **menu bar** of the **Snipping Tool** dialog box, click the **arrow** to the right of *New*—referred to as the **New arrow**—and then compare your screen with Figure 1.15.

An arrow attached to a button will display a menu when clicked. Such a button is referred to as a *split button*—clicking the main part of the button performs a command and clicking the arrow opens a menu with choices. A *menu* is a list of commands within a category, and a group of menus at the top of a program window is referred to as the *menu bar*.

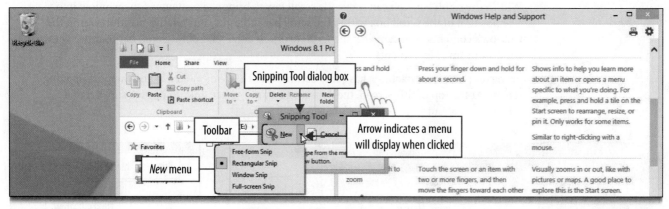

FIGURE 1.15

5 On the menu, notice that there are four types of snips.

A *free-form snip* lets you draw an irregular line, such as a circle, around an area of the screen. A *rectangular snip* lets you draw a precise box by dragging the mouse pointer around an area of the screen to form a rectangle. A *window snip* captures the entire displayed window. A *full-screen snip* captures the entire screen.

To *drag* is to move something from one location on the screen to another while holding down the left mouse button; the action of dragging includes releasing the mouse button at the desired time or location.

BY TOUCH   Slide your finger to drag and then lift your finger to release.

6 On the menu, click **Window Snip**. Then, move your mouse pointer over the open **Windows Help and Support** window, and notice that a red rectangle surrounds the window; the remainder of your screen dims.

7 With the ⟨🖑⟩ pointer positioned anywhere over the surrounded window, click the left mouse button one time. Use the scroll bar to position the snip near the top of the **Snipping Tool** window, and then compare your screen with Figure 1.16.

Your snip is copied to the Snipping Tool mark-up window. Here you can annotate—mark or make notes on—save, copy, or share the snip.

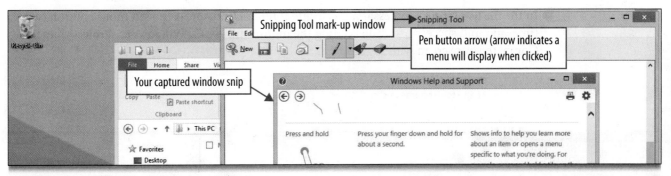

FIGURE 1.16

8 On the toolbar of the **Snipping Tool** mark-up window, click the **Pen button arrow** ✏, and then click **Red Pen**. Notice that your mouse pointer displays as a red dot.

9 In the illustration for *Pinch or stretch to zoom*, point to the left of one of the blue arrows, and then while holding down the left mouse button, draw a red free-form circle around the illustration. If you are not satisfied with your circle, on the toolbar, click the Eraser button ◨, point anywhere on the red circle, click to erase, and then begin again with Step 8.

10 On the toolbar of the **Snipping Tool** mark-up window, click the **Highlighter** ✏ button. Notice that your mouse pointer displays as a small yellow rectangle.

11 Point to the text *Pinch or stretch to zoom*, hold down the left mouse button, and then drag over the text to highlight it in yellow. If you are not satisfied with your yellow highlight, on the toolbar, click the Eraser button ◨, point anywhere on the yellow highlight, click to erase, and then begin again with Step 10. Compare your screen with Figure 1.17.

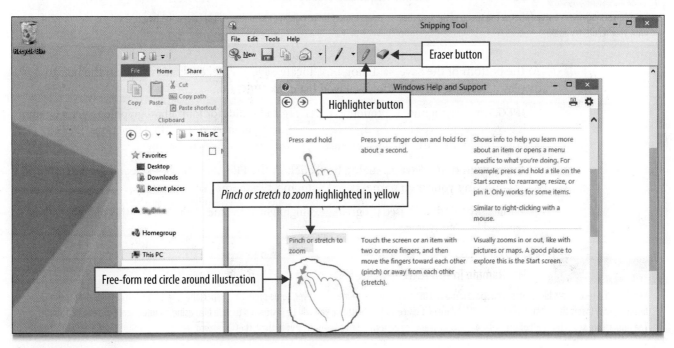

FIGURE 1.17

12 On the **Snipping Tool** mark-up window's toolbar, click **Save Snip** 💾 to display the **Save As** dialog box.

13 In the **Save As** dialog box, in the **navigation pane**, drag the scroll bar down as necessary to view **This PC**. Point to **This PC**, if necessary, click ▷ to expand the list, and then on the list, click the name of your **USB flash drive**.

14 In the **file list**, scroll as necessary, locate and *double-click*—press the left mouse button two times in rapid succession while holding the mouse still—your **Windows 8.1 Projects** folder. Compare your screen with Figure 1.18.

ANOTHER WAY   Right-click the folder name and click Open.

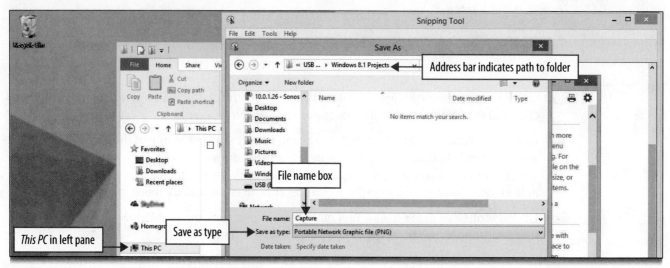

FIGURE 1.18

> **N O T E** **Successful Double-Clicking Requires a Steady Hand**
>
> Double-clicking needs a steady hand. The speed of the two clicks is not as important as holding the mouse still between the two clicks. If you are not satisfied with your result, try again.

15 At the bottom of the **Save As** dialog box, locate **Save as type**, click anywhere in the box to display a list, and then on the displayed list click **JPEG file**.

JPEG, which is commonly pronounced *JAY-peg* and stands for Joint Photographic Experts Group, is a common file type used by digital cameras and computers to store digital pictures. JPEG is popular because it can store a high-quality picture in a relatively small file.

16 At the bottom of the **Save As** dialog box, click in the **File name** box to select the text *Capture*, and then using your own name, type **Lastname_Firstname_1A_Zoom_Snip**

Within any Windows-based program, text highlighted in blue—selected—in this manner will be replaced by your typing.

> **N O T E** **File Naming in This Textbook**
>
> Windows 8.1 recognizes file names with spaces. You can use spaces in file names, however, some programs, especially when transferring files over the Internet, may insert the extra characters *%20* in place of a space. In this textbook you will be instructed to save files using an underscore instead of a space. The underscore key is the shift of the ⟨ - ⟩ key—on most keyboards located two or three keys to the left of ⟨Backspace⟩.

17 In the lower right corner of the window, click the **Save** button.

18 **Close** ❌ the **Snipping Tool** mark-up window, **Close** ❌ the **Windows Help and Support** window, and **Close** ❌ your **Windows 8.1 Projects** window. Hold this file until you finish Project 1A, and then submit as directed by your instructor.

You have successfully created a folder on a removable storage device and saved a file within that folder.

Apps Training
Video 1.2

Traditionally, the three major tasks of an operating system are to:

- Manage your computer's hardware—the printers, scanners, disk drives, monitors, and other hardware attached to it.
- Manage the application software installed on your computer—programs like those in Microsoft Office and other programs you might install to manage your money, edit photos, play games, and so on.
- Manage the *data* generated from your application software. Data refers to the documents, worksheets, pictures, songs, and so on that you create and store during the day-to-day use of your computer.

The Windows 8.1 operating system continues to perform these three tasks, and additionally is optimized for touchscreens; for example, tablets of all sizes and convertible laptop computers. Windows 8.1 works equally well with any input device, including a mouse, keyboard, touchscreen, and pen—a pen-shaped stylus that you tap on a computer screen.

The apps you use from the Start screen are referred to as *immersive*—they fill the screen with no borders. You can display more than one app on the screen at one time. This look and behavior of apps is called *modern design*, which refers to the design principles in Windows 8.1 that include tiles with white text on deeply colored backgrounds, consistent fonts, simpler navigation, and the use of the entire screen. The idea is that you are immersed in the app with few screen distractions.

In most instances, when you purchase a computer, the operating system software is already installed. The operating system consists of many smaller programs, stored as system files, which transfer data to and from the disk and transfer data in and out of your computer's memory. Other functions performed by the operating system include hardware-specific tasks such as checking to see if a key has been pressed on the keyboard and, if it has, displaying the appropriate letter or character on the screen.

When using a Windows 8.1 computer, you can write and create using traditional desktop apps, and you can also read and socialize and communicate by using the Windows Store apps. With Windows 8.1, as compared to earlier versions of Windows, your PC behaves like a smartphone or tablet—it is connected, it is mobile, and it is centered on people and activities. If, as Microsoft predicts, the laptop and tablet will ultimately merge into one device—like the Microsoft Surface shown in Figure 1.19—then you will be well prepared by learning to use Windows 8.1 and the Windows Store apps.

FIGURE 1.19

Windows 8.1, in the same manner as other operating systems and earlier versions of the Windows operating system, has a desktop that uses a *graphical user interface*—abbreviated as *GUI* and pronounced *GOO-ee*. A graphical user interface uses graphics such as an image of a file folder or wastebasket that you click to activate the item represented. A GUI commonly incorporates the following:

- A *pointer*—any symbol that displays on your screen in response to moving your mouse and with which you can select objects and commands.
- A *pointing device*, such as a mouse or touchpad, to control the pointer.
- *Icons*—small images that represent commands, files, applications, or other windows. By selecting an icon and pressing a mouse button, you can start a program or move objects to different locations on your screen.
- A *desktop*—a simulation of a real desk that represents your work area; here you can arrange icons, such as shortcuts to programs, files, folders, and various types of documents, in the same manner you would arrange physical objects on top of a desk.

In Windows 8.1, you now also have the Start screen, organized by tiles, that serves as a connected dashboard to all of your important sites, services, and apps. On the Start screen, your view is tailored to your information and activities; for example, pictures display as *thumbnails*—reduced images of graphics, email messages say who they are from, and videos include their length.

The physical parts of your computer such as the central processing unit (CPU), memory, and any attached devices such as a printer, are collectively known as *resources*. The operating system keeps track of the status of each resource and decides when a resource needs attention and for how long.

There will be times when you want and need to interact with the functions of the operating system; for example, when you want to install a new hardware device like a color printer. Windows 8.1 provides tools with which you can inform the operating system of new hardware that you attach to your computer.

Software application programs are the programs that enable you to do work on, and be entertained by, your computer—programs such as Word and Excel found in the Microsoft Office suite of products, Adobe Photoshop, and computer games. An application program, however, cannot run on its own—it must run under the direction of the operating system.

For the everyday use of your computer, the most important and most often used function of the operating system is managing your files and folders—referred to as *data management* or *file management*. In the same manner that you strive to keep your paper documents and file folders organized so that you can find information when you need it, your goal when organizing your computer files and folders is to group your files so that you can find information easily. Managing your data files so that you can find your information when you need it is an important computing skill.

To check how well you can identify operating system functions, take a moment to answer the following questions:

1. Of the three major functions of the operating system, the first is to manage your computer's _____ such as disk drives, monitors, and printers.

2. The second major function of the operating system is to manage the application _____ such as Microsoft Word, Microsoft Excel, and video games.

3. The third major function of the operating system is to manage the _____ generated from your applications—the files such as Word documents, Excel workbooks, pictures, and songs.

4. The Start screen, which displays live tiles with your updated information, is your connected _____ to all of your important sites and services.

5. An important computer skill to learn is how to manage your _____ _____ so that you can find your information quickly.

Apps Training
Video 1.3

According to Microsoft, a billion people in the world use Windows and 93% of PCs in the world run some version of Windows. Increasingly people want to use Windows in a format that runs easily on mobile computing devices such as laptops, tablets, and convertibles; research shows this is where people now spend more time.

With only desktop apps to choose from, Windows is centered around files—typing and creating things—and that will continue to be an important part of what you do on your computer. Additionally, you are doing different kinds of things on your PC, and you probably expect your PC to be more like a smartphone—connected all the time, mobile, to have long battery life if your PC is a laptop, and be centered on the people and activities that are important to you. It is for those activities that the Windows Store apps—also referred to as *Windows apps*—will become important to you.

Think of Windows 8.1 as a way to do work on your desktop or laptop computer, and then to read and be entertained on your laptop, tablet, or Xbox game console. Microsoft promotes Windows 8.1 as both serious—for work, and fun—for entertainment and social networking.

Activity 1.07 | Using Windows Store Apps

An array of Windows Store apps displays on the Start screen immediately after you sign in to a Windows 8.1 computer. On a new computer, the apps might be preselected by your computer manufacturer and by Microsoft. You can use these right away, and later you can add, delete, and rearrange the apps so that your Start screen becomes your own personal dashboard. Recall that some apps are represented by live tiles that will update with your personal information, such as Mail, after you set them to do so.

1 With your **desktop** still displayed, in the lower left corner, click **Start** ⊞.

You can use this technique to return to the Start screen from any other screen—including the desktop.

2 On your **Start screen**, locate and point to the **Sports** app tile that comes with Windows 8.1. If necessary, point to the bottom of the screen, and then drag the scroll bar to the right to locate the app. If you cannot locate the Sports app, select some other news app. Compare your screen with Figure 1.20.

BY TOUCH To display the Start screen, swipe in from the right and tap Start. To scroll, slide your finger to the left to scroll to the right.

FIGURE 1.20

3 Click the **Sports** app tile, if necessary wait a moment if this is the first time you have used this app, point anywhere on the screen, and then right-click to display the app bar. Compare your screen with Figure 1.21.

This feature is the ***app bar***—an area at the top or bottom of a Windows Store app containing various controls pertaining to the app. Here you can navigate directly to categories such as the NBA (National Basketball Association) or MLB (Major League Baseball).

 BY TOUCH On a touchscreen, from the bottom or top of the screen, swipe slightly upward or downward to display the app bar.

 **ANOTHER WAY** Press 🪟 + Z to display the app bar in an app.

FIGURE 1.21

4 At the top of the screen, to right of **HOME**, click the **arrow**, and then click **Favorite Teams**. Click **Add** ⊕. With the **insertion point** blinking in the **Add to Favorite Teams** box type **Los** and then compare your screen with Figure 1.22.

The ***insertion point*** is a blinking vertical line that indicates where text will be inserted when you type.

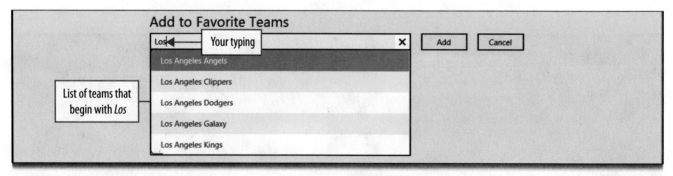

FIGURE 1.22

5 On the list, click **Los Angeles Dodgers**, and then compare your screen with Figure 1.23.

Depending on the time of year and the team's standing, the information will vary.

FAVORITE TEAMS

Enter a team or player name

Los Angeles Dodgers
1st in NL West

92-70, L 2

Team information (yours will vary)

+

FIGURE 1.23

6 On your keyboard, in the lower left corner, locate and then press ⊞ to display the **Start screen**.

This is the keyboard technique to display the Start screen.

7 On the **Start screen**, click the **Sports** app tile again.

The Favorite Teams screen with your selected team information displays because this was the last screen displayed before you returned to the Start screen.

8 On the **Favorite Teams** screen, click the **Los Angeles Dodgers** tile. Move your mouse slightly to display the gray scroll bar at the bottom of the screen, and then drag the scroll box to the right to see news stories related to the Los Angeles Dodgers.

⟳ **BY TOUCH**   Slide your finger to the left to scroll to the right to view more articles.

9 Point to the top of the screen to display the title bar, and then on the right end of the title bar, click ✕ to close the Sports app and return to the desktop.

Use this technique to close an app. Leaving an app, for example by pressing ⊞ to redisplay the Start screen, does not close it. In Windows 8.1, the default behavior is to return to the desktop after closing an app; however, you can change this behavior to return to the Start screen instead. These settings can be found in the Taskbar and Navigation Properties dialog box.

⟳ **BY TOUCH**   Swipe from the top of the screen to the bottom of the screen to close the app.

10 Press ⊞ or click the Start button ⊞ to redisplay the **Start screen**, and then click the **Maps** app tile. If necessary, click Allow if prompted to use your location. Then press ⊞ to return to the **Start screen**.

11 With the **Start screen** redisplayed, locate and then click the **Finance** app tile. Right-click anywhere on the screen, and then at the top, click the **WATCHLIST** tile. Click **Add** ⊕, and then in the **Add to Watchlist** box type **Microsoft** Click **Add** to add the NASDAQ stock listing for Microsoft. If Microsoft is already on your WATCHLIST, click Cancel.

A WATCHLIST tile for Microsoft Corporation, displaying their stock symbol MSFT, displays the latest information about Microsoft's stock price. Other companies might also display on your WATCHLIST.

12 Click **MSFT** to see a graph of the day's stock price. At the bottom, click **1 Year** to see a graph representing one year.

13 With your Microsoft graph displayed, press and hold down [⊞] and press [PrintScrn] and then release the two keys. Notice that your screen dims momentarily; you will view the screenshot at the end of this activity.

> A *keyboard shortcut* is a combination of two or more keyboard keys, used to perform a task that would otherwise require a mouse.

> On the Start screen or in a Windows Store app, use this technique to create a screenshot. Snipping Tool is not available for the Start screen or Windows Store apps. The screenshot file is automatically stored in your Pictures folder of This PC.

14 Move the mouse slightly to display the gray scroll bar at the bottom of the screen, and then drag the scroll box to the right to view the latest news stories about Microsoft.

15 Press [⊞] to redisplay the **Start screen**.

> From any screen, recall that you can redisplay the Start screen by pointing to the lower left corner and clicking [⊞] or by pressing [⊞].

16 Locate and then click the **Food & Drink** app tile. Move your mouse slightly to display the gray scroll bar at the bottom of the screen, and then drag the scroll box to the right to display pictures of featured articles and recipes.

17 Use one of the techniques you have practiced to redisplay the **Start screen**, and then point to the upper left corner of your screen. Notice a thumbnail of the last app you used—the Food & Drink app. Compare your screen with Figure 1.24.

> This corner displays a thumbnail image of the last screen you were on, and you can use it to *go back* to your previous screen.

Most recently displayed app (your image will differ)

Start   Firstname
                                         Lastname

Faint lines indicate other apps that are open

FIGURE 1.24

18 With the thumbnail displayed, notice faint vertical lines directly below and along the left edge of the screen. Without holding down any mouse buttons, point to the extreme upper left corner of the displayed thumbnail and quickly move the mouse down the extreme left edge of the screen to display thumbnail images of the other open apps. Compare your screen with Figure 1.25.

> This is the thumbnail view of open apps that displays when you move your mouse down from the upper left corner. To switch to an app that is still open, you can click any of the thumbnails.

Food & Drink

Finance

Open apps, including Desktop
(your images will vary)

Maps

FIGURE 1.25

ANOTHER WAY   Hold down [⊞] and press [Tab] to display the thumbnails of open apps. Continue to hold down [⊞] to keep the display open. Click any displayed app to move to it.

19 Point to the thumbnail of the **Finance** app, right-click, and then click **Close**.

Use this technique to close an app without redisplaying it.

20 Use the same technique to close the **Maps** app and the **Food & Drink** app.

More **Knowledge**   **Rotate among open apps**

Click the thumbnail image in the upper left corner to open the app, and then click the next image in the upper left corner to rotate among open apps.

Activity 1.08 | **Moving Between the Start Screen and Desktop and Saving a Windows Store App Screenshot as a File**

In the day-to-day use of your computer, depending on what you need to do, you will move between desktop apps and Windows Store apps, and it is easy to do so.

1 Display your **Start screen**, locate the **Desktop** tile and click it one time.

If you move frequently from the Start screen to the desktop, you will want to keep your desktop tile easily visible.

ANOTHER WAY   From any Windows Store app or the Start screen, point to the Start button in the lower left corner of the screen, right-click, and then on the shortcut menu, click Desktop.

---

2 From the taskbar, open **File Explorer** 📁 to display the **This PC** window. In the **file list**, double-click **Pictures**, and then double-click **Screenshots**—this navigation is typically indicated as **This PC ▶ Pictures ▶ Screenshots**. On the ribbon, click the **View** tab, and then in the **Layout group**, if necessary, click **Large icons**. Compare your screen with Figure 1.26.

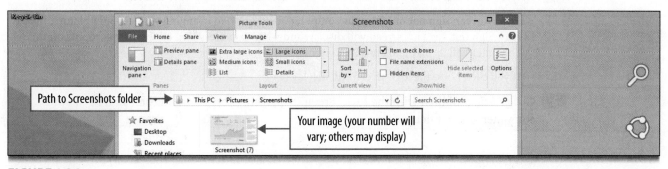

FIGURE 1.26

3 In the **file list**, click one time to select the **Screenshot** file that you captured of the Microsoft graph; if more than one Screenshot file displays, click to select the file that has the highest number.

A screenshot captured in this manner from a Windows Store app is saved as a *.png* file, which is commonly pronounced *PING*, and stands for Portable Network Graphic. This is an image file type that can be transferred over the Internet.

4 On the ribbon, on the **Home tab**, in the **Organize group**, click **Rename**, and then using your own name, type **Lastname_Firstname_1A_Graph_Snip** Press Enter.

5 With the renamed file selected, on the ribbon, in the **Organize group**, click **Move to**, and then at the bottom of the list, click **Choose location**. In the **Move Items** dialog box, scroll to locate your USB drive, double-click to expand the drive, and then double-click your **Windows 8.1 Projects** folder. With the name of your folder highlighted in blue, click **Move**.

Hold this file until you complete Project 1A.

6 **Close** ☒ the **Screenshots** window.

Objective 4 | Sign Out of Windows 8.1 and Turn Off Your Computer

Apps Training
Video 1.4

On your own computer, when you are done working, sign out from Windows 8.1, and then set your computer properly so that your data is saved, you save energy, and your computer remains secure.

When you turn off your computer by using the *Sleep* command, Windows 8.1 automatically saves your work, the screen goes dark, the computer's fan stops, and your computer goes to sleep. You need not close your programs or files because your work is saved. When you wake your computer by pressing a key, moving the mouse, or using whatever method is appropriate for your device, your screen will display exactly like it did when you turned off your computer.

When you *shut down* your computer, all open programs and files close, network connections close, and the hard disk stops. No power is used. According to Microsoft, about half of all Windows users like to shut down so that they get a "fresh start" each time they turn on the computer. The other half use sleep.

Activity 1.09 | Locking, Signing Out of, and Shutting Down Your Computer

In an organization, there might be a specific process for signing out from Windows 8.1 and turning off the computer.

1 Display the **Start screen**. In the upper right corner, click your user name.

Here you can sign out or lock your computer, in addition to changing your account picture. If you click Sign out, the lock screen will display, and when you press Enter, all the user accounts on this computer will display and are able to sign in.

If you click Lock, the lock screen will display.

2 Click **Lock**, and then with the lock screen displayed, press Enter, and then sign in to your computer again if necessary.

3 On the **Start screen**, point to the upper right corner of the screen to display the charms in a transparent view, and then move the mouse downward slightly into the displayed symbols along the right edge of the screen to display the **charms** in an opaque overlay. Compare your screen with Figure 1.27.

Charms are a specific and consistent set of buttons that you can use in every app, whether a Windows Store app or a desktop app, and they enable you to search, share, access devices, or adjust your PC settings. Specifically you can:

- Use the Search charm to search your computer, your apps, and the Internet.
- Use the Share charm to send links, photos, screenshots, and other content to your friends and social networks—provided that you have installed the appropriate apps—without leaving the app you are in.
- Use the Start charm to go directly to the Start screen, or from the Start screen to the last app that you were using.
- Use the Devices charm to connect to devices and send content, stream media, and print.
- Use the Settings charm to perform basic tasks like shutting down your PC, changing volume and brightness, and configuring account settings.

FIGURE 1.27

4 Click the **Settings charm**, and then compare your screen with Figure 1.28.

FIGURE 1.28

5 At the bottom of the **Settings pane**, click **Power**, and then click **Shut down**.

Objective 5 | Customize and Manage User Accounts

Apps Training
Video 1.5

Windows 8.1 supports multiple local account users on a single computer, and at least one user is the administrator—the initial administrator that was established when the system was purchased or when Windows 8.1 was installed.

As the administrator of your own computer, you can restrict access to your computer so that only people you authorize can use your computer or view its files. This access is managed through a local *user account*, which is a collection of information that tells Windows 8.1 what files and folders the account holder can access, what changes the account holder can make to the computer system, and what the account holder's personal preferences are. Each person accesses his or her user account with a user name and password, and each user has his or her own desktop, files, and folders. Users with a local account should also establish a Microsoft account so that their Start screen arrangement—personal dashboard of tiles—roams with them when they sign on to other Windows 8.1 computers.

An *administrator account* allows complete access to the computer. Administrators can make changes that affect other users, change security settings, install software and hardware, access all files on the computer, and make changes to other user accounts.

Activity 1.10 | **Changing How Your Desktop Displays on Startup and Viewing the Apps on the Taskbar**

1 If necessary, turn on or wake your computer, sign in, and then display your **Desktop**.

2 Point to an empty area of the taskbar, right-click, and then on the shortcut menu, click **Properties**.

26 **Windows 8.1** | Chapter 1: Getting Started with Windows 8.1

3 In the **Taskbar and Navigation properties** dialog box, click the **Navigation tab**, and then compare your screen with Figure 1.29.

Here you can change the corner navigation; however, most Windows 8.1 users will probably leave the default settings for corner navigation.

🔄 **BY TOUCH**   Press briefly on the taskbar until a white square displays, and then release your finger to display the shortcut menu. Tap Properties, and then tap the Navigation tab.

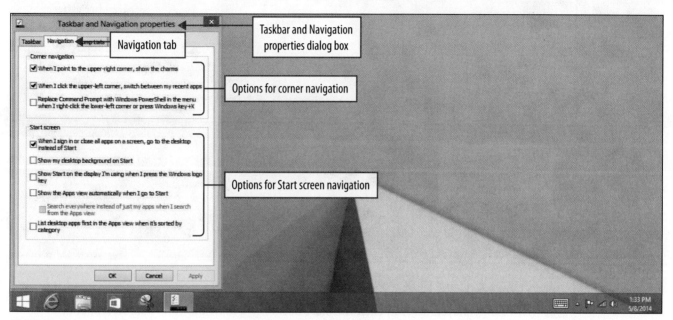

FIGURE 1.29

4 Under **Start screen**, take a few moments to study the properties.

On desktop or laptop PCs where a keyboard and mouse are connected, this property is selected by default, which means you will go directly to the desktop when you sign in to your computer. If you use desktop apps for most of your computing, for example Office or PhotoShop, you might prefer this setting, which bypasses the Start screen. Additionally, if you display the Start screen and use one or more apps, upon closing all apps, the desktop will redisplay. On tablet devices, this property is not set as a default.

If you select the second check box, the background of your desktop will also become the background for your Start screen. Some computer users prefer this, because it makes transitioning between the desktop and Start screen look smoother and less dramatic. On the other hand, some computer users like the different backgrounds.

The third check box applies to situations where you have multiple monitors attached to your PC. When checked, you can move your mouse into the display you want to look at, click, and then press the Windows logo key to show the Start screen on that display.

If you select the fourth check box, the Start screen will automatically display in the *Apps view* instead of the default tiles view. Apps view displays a small tile of the same size for all apps.

If you select the fifth check box, the Apps view on the Start screen will list desktop apps first when the Apps view is sorted by category.

5 **Close** ✖ the **Taskbar and Navigation properties** dialog box. Click the **Start** button ⊞, locate and click the **Weather** app, and if necessary, allow the app to use your location. Move your mouse to the lower edge of the screen until the taskbar displays. Notice that the icon for the Weather app displays on your taskbar. Compare your screen with Figure 1.30.

In the Windows Store apps, you can still view the taskbar by moving your mouse to the lower edge of the screen.

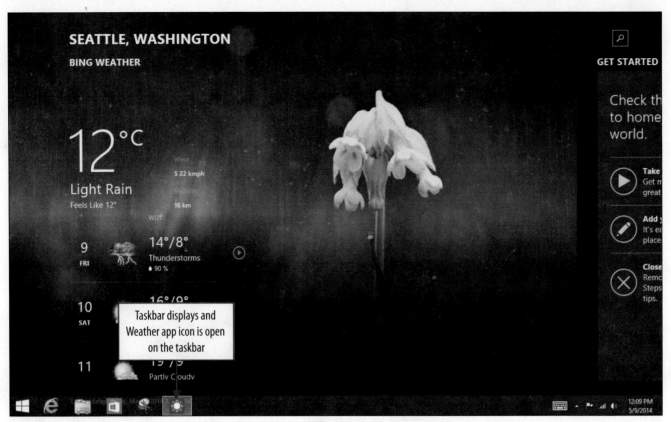

FIGURE 1.30

6 ▷ On your displayed taskbar, click the **Start** button ▦ to display the **Start screen**, and then click the Desktop tile. On the taskbar, point to the Weather app icon to display the thumbnail. Compare your screen with Figure 1.31.

Windows Store apps that you open also display on the taskbar on the desktop. Here you can redisplay the app; or, you can right-click the app icon and choose to pin the app to your taskbar, which is convenient for apps you use frequently such as Weather or Mail or Facebook.

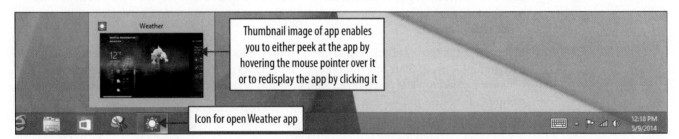

FIGURE 1.31

7 ▷ Press ⊞ to return to the **Start screen**. Point to the upper left corner of the Start screen, move the mouse down quickly, right-click the thumbnail image of the open Weather app, and then click **Close**.

8 ▷ In the upper right corner of the Start screen, to the right of your name, click the Power button, and if you want to do so, shut down your computer. As directed by your instructor, submit the two files that are the results of this project.

END | You have completed Project 1A

Managing Files and Folders

PROJECT ACTIVITIES

In Activities 1.11 through 1.21, you will assist Barbara Hewitt and Steven Ramos, who work for the Information Technology Department at the Boston headquarters office of the Bell Orchid Hotels. Barbara and Steven have been asked to organize some of the files and folders that comprise the corporation's computer data. You will capture screens that will look similar to Figure 1.32.

PROJECT FILES

For Project 1B, you will need the following files:

The student data files that accompany this textbook stored on a USB flash drive

You will save your files as:

Lastname_Firstname_1B_WordPad_Snip
Lastname_Firstname_1B_Europe_Folders_Snip
Lastname_Firstname_1B_HR_Snip

PROJECT RESULTS

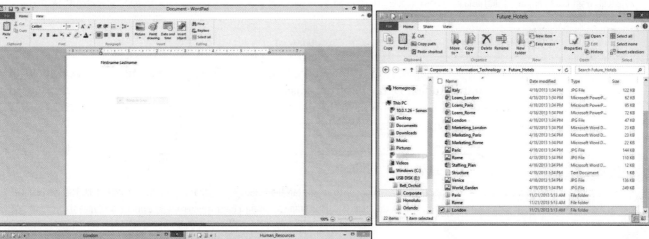

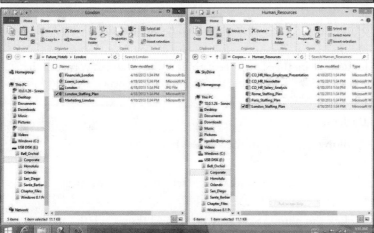

FIGURE 1.32 Project 1B Managing Files and Folders

Apps Training
Video 1.6

A file is the fundamental unit of storage that enables Windows 8.1 to distinguish one set of information from another. A folder is the basic organizing tool for files. In a folder, you can store files that are related to one another. You can also put a folder inside of another folder, which is referred to as a subfolder.

Windows 8.1 arranges folders in a structure that resembles a *hierarchy*—an arrangement where items are ranked and where each level is lower in rank than the item above it. The hierarchy of folders is referred to as the *folder structure*. A sequence of folders in the folder structure that leads to a specific file or folder is a path.

A library gathers folders that are stored in different locations so you can browse them in one place. A library does not actually store your items; rather, a library provides a single access point from which you can open folders and files from different locations. In the navigation pane, libraries are hidden by default, but you can view them by opening Desktop under Favorites.

ALERT!

For the remainder of this textbook, you will need two of the folders that accompany this textbook. You will download these files in the following activity. Alternatively, your instructor might provide these folders, or you can download the files from the Pearson website associated with this textbook. You will also need Microsoft Office 2013 (only Word, Excel, and PowerPoint) installed on the computer you are using. A trial version of Microsoft Office 2013 is sufficient for these projects.

Activity 1.11 | Downloading Files from a Website

To complete this chapter, you will need the Bell Orchid Files and the Chapter Files, which are included in the Student Data Files from this book's website. Follow the steps in this activity to download these files to your USB flash drive. Alternatively, your instructor might provide these folders to you, for example in your learning management system.

NOTE | **Using a Touchscreen**

If you are using a touchscreen computer to complete this project, continue to use the tap and swipe gestures that you practiced in Project 1A. The remainder of this textbook will assume a mouse and keyboard setup, but all the projects can be completed using a touchscreen without a mouse or keyboard.

---

1 ▶ Sign in to your computer, and then from the **Start screen**, display the **desktop**.

There are several ways to display the desktop from the Start screen when using a mouse and keyboard. You can click the desktop tile on the Start screen, point to the lower left corner of the screen and click the Start button, press [⊞] + [D], or point to the lower left corner, right-click, and then at the bottom of the menu click Desktop.

2 ▶ If necessary, insert your **USB flash drive**.

3 ▶ On the taskbar, click **Internet Explorer** [e], click in the **address bar**, type **www.pearsonhighered.com/go** and then press [Enter].

Internet Explorer is Microsoft's *web browser*—software with which you display webpages and navigate the Internet.

4 ▶ Scroll down the list, locate and click the name of this textbook, and then click the **STUDENT DATA FILES tab**.

5 ▶ Click the link for **Bell Orchid Files**. In the **Internet Explorer** dialog box, click **Save as**.

Recall that a dialog box is a small window that displays options for completing a task.

6 ▶ In the **Save As** dialog box, in the **navigation pane** on the left, scroll down, and if necessary, to the left of **This PC**, click ▷ to expand the list. Then click the name of your **USB flash drive**. Compare your screen with Figure 1.33.

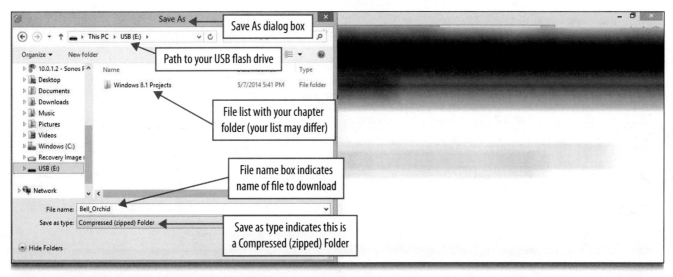

FIGURE 1.33

> **7** In the lower right corner, click **Save**.

At the bottom of your screen, the *Notification bar* displays information about pending downloads, security issues, add-ons, and other issues related to the operation of your computer.

A *compressed file* is a file that has been reduced in size. Compressed files take up less storage space and can be transferred to other computers faster than uncompressed files. You can also combine a group of files into one compressed folder, which makes it easier to share a group of files.

> **8** At the bottom of the screen, in the **Notification bar**, when the download is complete, click **Open folder**, and then compare your screen with Figure 1.34.

FIGURE 1.34

> **9** With the compressed folder selected, on the ribbon, click the **Extract tab** to display the **Compressed Folder Tools**, and then click **Extract all**. Compare your screen with Figure 1.35.

Here you *extract*—decompress, or pull out—files from a compressed form. When you extract, an uncompressed copy is placed in the folder that you specify here.

You can navigate to some other location by clicking the Browse button and navigating within your storage locations.

ALERT!	File Explorer Displays Check Boxes on Touchscreen Systems

On touchscreen systems, File Explorer displays check boxes to the left of file and folder names to make it easier to select items by touch or with a stylus. If you are not working with a touchscreen, you will not see these check boxes.

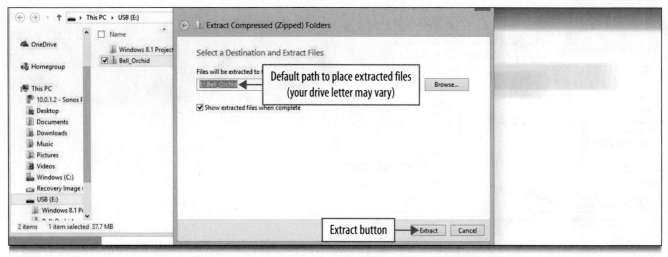

FIGURE 1.35

10 ▶ Click the **Browse** button. In the **Select a destination** dialog box, click **This PC**, scroll down as necessary and click the name of your **USB flash drive**, and then click **OK**.

11 ▶ In the lower right corner, click **Extract**. Notice that a progress bar indicates the progress of the extract process, and that when the extract is complete, the **Bell_Orchid** folder displays in the file list of your **USB flash drive**. If you want to do so, you can delete the compressed (zipped) folder from your flash drive because now you have an extracted *copy* of the folder.

> In a dialog box or taskbar button, a **progress bar** indicates visually the progress of a task such as a download or file transfer.

12 ▶ When complete, in the upper right corner of the **USB** window, click **Close** ⊠.

13 ▶ Using the techniques you just practiced, return to the website if necessary, and then download and extract the Chapter Files to your USB flash drive. Then delete the compressed folder if you want to do so. **Close** ⊠ all open windows and redisplay your desktop.

Activity 1.12 | Using File Explorer to Display Locations, Folders, and Files

Recall that File Explorer is the program that displays the contents of locations, folders, and files on your computer, and also enables you to perform tasks related to your files and folders such as copying, moving, and renaming. When you open a folder or location, a window displays to show its contents. The design of the window helps you navigate—explore within the folder structure for the purpose of finding files and folders—so that you can save and locate your files and folders efficiently.

In this activity, you will open a folder and examine the parts of its window.

1 ▶ With your desktop displayed, on the taskbar, *point to* but do not click **File Explorer** 📁, and notice the ScreenTip *File Explorer*.

> A **ScreenTip** displays useful information when you perform various mouse actions, such as pointing to screen elements.

2 Click **File Explorer** 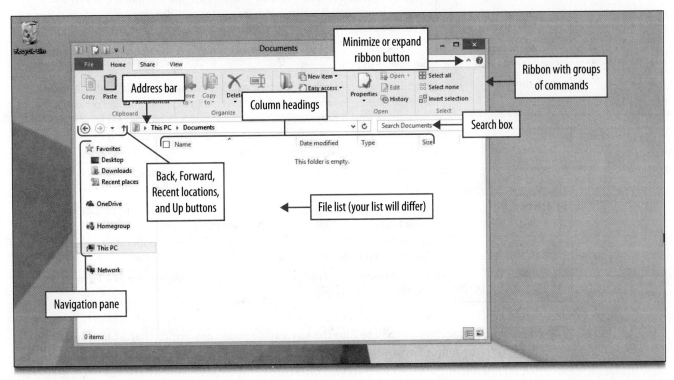 to display the **This PC** window.

File Explorer is at work anytime you are viewing the contents of a location, a folder, or a file.

By default, the File Explorer button on the taskbar opens to This PC. Here you have a folder for Documents, Music, Pictures, Videos, Desktop, and Downloads.

3 In the **file list**, click **Documents** one time to select it, and then on the ribbon, on the **Computer tab**, in the **Location group**, click **Open**.

The window for the Documents folder displays. You may or may not have files and folders already stored here.

ANOTHER WAY   Point to Documents, right-click to display a shortcut menu, and then click Open; or, point to Documents and double-click.

---

4 Compare your screen with Figure 1.36, and then take a moment to study the parts of the window as described in the table in Figure 1.37.

FIGURE 1.36

FIGURE 1.37

PARTS OF THE DOCUMENTS WINDOW	
WINDOW PART	**FUNCTION**
Address bar	Displays your current location in the file structure as a series of links separated by arrows. Tap or click a part of the path to go to that level or tap or click at the end to select the path for copying.
Back, Forward, Recent locations, and Up buttons	Provides the ability to navigate to other folders you have already opened without closing the current window. These buttons work with the address bar; that is, after you use the address bar to change folders, you can use the Back button to return to the original folder. Use the Up button to open the location where the folder you are viewing is saved—also referred to as the *parent folder*.
Column headings	Identify the columns. By clicking the column heading name, you can change how the files in the file list are organized; by clicking the arrow on the right, you can select various sort arrangements in the file list. Right-click a column heading to select other columns to display in the file list.
File list	Displays the contents of the current folder. If you type text into the Search box, only the folders and files that match your search will display here—including files in subfolders.
Minimize or expand ribbon button	Changes the display of the ribbon. When minimized, the ribbon shows only the tab names and not the full ribbon.
Navigation pane	Displays locations to which you can navigate; for example, your OneDrive, folders on your PC, devices and drives connected to your PC, Favorites, and other PCs on your network. Use Favorites to open your most commonly used folders and searches. If you have a folder that you use frequently, you can drag it to the Favorites area so that it is easily accessible.
Ribbon	Groups common tasks such as copying and moving, creating new folders, emailing and zipping items, and changing views on related tabs.
Search box	Enables you to type a word or phrase and then searches for a file or subfolder stored in the current folder that contains matching text. The search begins as soon as you begin typing; for example, if you type *G*, all the files that start with the letter *G* display in the file list.
Status bar	Displays the total number of items in a location, or the number of selected items and their total size.

5 ▶ Move your ⬚ pointer anywhere into the **navigation pane**, and notice that a **black arrow** (◢) displays to the left of *Favorites* to indicate that this item is expanded, and a **white arrow** (▷) displays to the left of items that are collapsed.

You can click these arrows to collapse and expand areas in the navigation pane.

6 ▶ In the **navigation pane**, if necessary expand **This PC**, and then click your **USB flash drive** one time to display its contents in the **file list**. Compare your screen with Figure 1.38.

In the navigation pane, *This PC* displays all of the drive letter locations attached to your computer, including the internal hard drives, CD or DVD drives, and any connected devices such as a USB flash drive.

The ribbon adds a *Drive Tools* contextual tab to provide commands you might need when working with various drives on your computer.

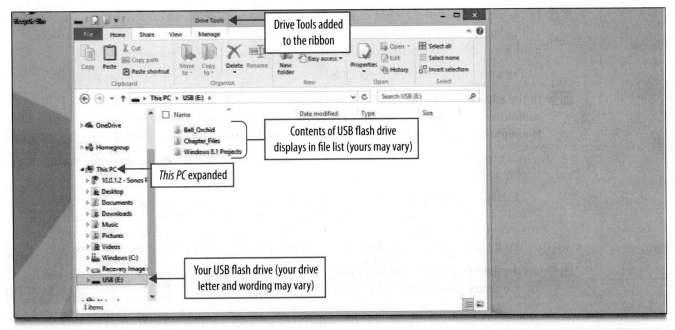

FIGURE 1.38

7 In the **file list**, double-click the **Bell_Orchid** folder—*not* the compressed folder if you have not deleted it to display its subfolders.

Recall that the corporate office of the Bell Orchid Hotels is in Boston. The corporate office maintains subfolders labeled for each of its large hotels in Honolulu, Orlando, San Diego, and Santa Barbara.

 **ANOTHER WAY**   Right-click the folder, and then click Open; or, select the folder and then on the ribbon click Open.

8 In the **file list**, double-click **Orlando** to display the subfolders, and then look at the **address bar** to view the path. Compare your screen with Figure 1.39.

Within each city's subfolder, there is a structure of subfolders for the Accounting, Engineering, Food and Beverage, Human Resources, Operations, and Sales and Marketing departments.

Because folders can be placed inside of other folders, such an arrangement is common when organizing files on a computer.

In the address bar, the path from the flash drive to the chapter folder to the Bell_Orchid folder to the Orlando folder displays as a series of links.

FIGURE 1.39

9 In the **address bar**, to the right of **Bell_Orchid**, click the ▶ arrow to display a list of the subfolders in the **Bell_Orchid** folder. On the list that displays, notice that **Orlando** displays in bold, indicating it is open in the file list. Then, on the list, click **Honolulu**.

The subfolders within the Honolulu folder display.

10 In the **address bar**, to the right of **Bell_Orchid**, click the ▶ arrow again to display the subfolders in the **Bell_Orchid** folder. Then, on the **address bar** (not on the list), point to **Honolulu** and notice that the list of subfolders in the **Honolulu** folder displays.

After you display one set of subfolders in the address bar, all of the links are active and you need only point to them to display the list of subfolders.

Clicking an arrow to the right of a folder name in the address bar displays a list of the subfolders in that folder. You can click a subfolder name to display its contents. In this manner, the address bar is not only a path, but it is also an active control with which you can step from the current folder directly to any other folder above it in the folder structure just by clicking on a folder name.

11 On the list of subfolders for **Honolulu**, click **Sales_Marketing** to display its contents in the file list. Compare your screen with Figure 1.40.

↻ ANOTHER WAY In the list, double-click the Sales_Marketing folder.

The files in the Sales_Marketing folder for Honolulu display. To the left of each file name, an icon indicates the program that created each file. Here, there is one PowerPoint file, one Excel file, one Word file, and four JPEG images.

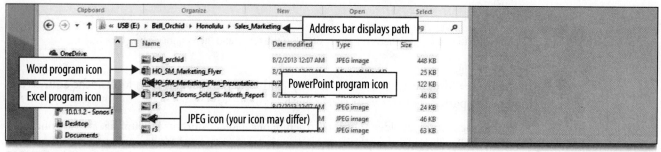

FIGURE 1.40

12 In the upper left portion of the window, click the **Back** button ⬅.

The Back button retraces each of your clicks in the same manner as clicking the Back button when you are browsing the Internet.

13 In the **file list**, point to the **Human_Resources** folder, and double-click to open the folder.

14 In the **file list**, click one time to select the PowerPoint file **HO_HR_New_Employee_Presentation**, and then on the ribbon, click the **View tab**. In the **Panes group**, click **Details pane**. In the **Show/hide group**, notice that **Item check boxes** is selected. Compare your screen with Figure 1.41.

The **Details pane** displays the most common **file properties** associated with the selected file. File properties refer to information about a file, such as the author, the date the file was last changed, and any descriptive **tags**—properties that you create to help you find and organize your files.

On touchscreen systems, such as the one used in this book, the Item check boxes feature is selected by default. Displaying the small check boxes to the right of file names makes it easier to select them by touch. If you like this feature, on non-touch systems, you can turn it on here.

Additionally, a thumbnail of the first slide in the presentation displays.

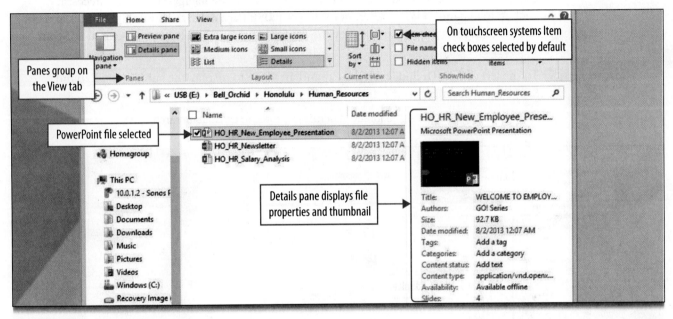

FIGURE 1.41

15 On the ribbon, in the **Panes group**, click **Preview pane** to replace the **Details pane** with the **Preview pane**. Compare your screen with Figure 1.42.

In the Preview pane that displays on the right, you can use the scroll bar to scroll through the slides in the presentation; or, you can click the up or down scroll arrow to view the slides.

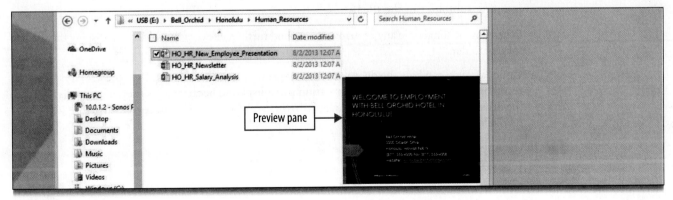

FIGURE 1.42

16 On the ribbon, click **Preview pane** to close the right pane completely. **Close** ☒ the window.

Use the Details pane to see a file's properties and the Preview pane when you want to look at a file quickly without actually opening it.

Activity 1.13 | Using the Navigation Pane to Display the Folder Structure

When it is useful to do so, you can use the navigation pane to navigate to files and folders and to display the folder structure.

1 If necessary, **Close** ☒ any open windows, and then on the taskbar, click **File Explorer** 🗔 to open the **This PC** window.

2 On the left side of the window, in the lower portion of the **navigation pane**, if necessary click ▷ to expand **This PC**. Then point to your **USB flash drive** containing your files and click the white expand arrow ▷ to display the subfolders immediately below the name of your USB drive.

3 To the left of **Bell_Orchid**, click the expand arrow ▷ to display the subfolders. Expand **San_Diego**. Compare your screen with Figure 1.43.

In the navigation pane, the folder structure is shown in a visual hierarchy.

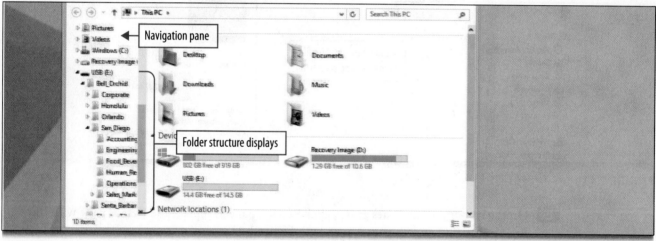

FIGURE 1.43

4 In the **navigation pane**, under **San_Diego**, click **Accounting** to display the files in the **Accounting** subfolder in the **file list**.

When you no longer see any ▷ arrows to expand further, clicking the folder will display the file list for that folder.

Optionally you can hide the display of the navigation pane, also referred to as the *left pane*, but it is recommended that you leave the navigation pane displayed because of its usefulness in displaying the drives on your computer and the folder structure when you want to see the structure in a hierarchical view.

5 In the upper right corner, click **Close** ☒.

Apps Training
Video 1.7

When you are using the software programs installed on your computer, you create and save data files—the documents, workbooks, databases, songs, pictures, and so on that you need for your job or personal use. Therefore, most of your work with Windows 8.1 desktop apps is concerned with locating and starting your programs and locating and opening your files.

You can start programs from the Start screen or from the desktop by pinning a program to the taskbar. You can open your data files from within the program in which they were created, or you can open a data file from a window in File Explorer, which will simultaneously start the program and open your file.

> **NOTE** | **You Need Microsoft Word 2013**
>
> To complete this project you need Microsoft Word 2013; you can use a trial version if necessary.

Activity 1.14 | Starting Programs and Opening Data Files

1 With your desktop displayed, use any technique that you have practiced to display the **Start screen**, and then type **paint**

Recall that from the Start screen, you can begin typing and the search feature will immediately begin searching your PC and the web.

Paint is a desktop app that comes with Windows 8.1 with which you can create and edit drawings and display and edit stored photos.

2 With the **Paint** app in focus—shaded—as the result of your search, press Enter to open the desktop app.

3 On the ribbon, with the **Home tab** active, in the **Tools group**, click the **Pencil** icon. Move your mouse pointer into the white drawing area, hold down the left mouse button, and then try drawing the letters of your first name in the white area of the window.

> **⟳ BY TOUCH**   Use your finger to draw on the screen.

4 In the upper left corner, to the left of the **Home tab**, click the **File tab** to display a menu of commands of things you can do with your picture.

5 On the menu, click **Exit**. In the displayed message, click **Don't Save**.

Messages like this display in most programs to prevent you from forgetting to save your work. A file saved in the Paint program creates a graphic file in the JPEG format.

6 Return to the **Start screen**, type **wordpad** and then open the WordPad desktop app. Notice that this program window has characteristics similar to the Paint program window; for example, it has a ribbon of commands.

7 With the insertion point blinking in the document window, type your first and last name.

8 From the taskbar, start **Snipping Tool**, and then create a **Window Snip**. Click anywhere in the WordPad window to display the **Snipping Tool** mark-up window. **Save** the snip as a **JPEG** in your **Windows 8.1 Projects** folder as **Lastname_Firstname_1B_WordPad_Snip** Hold this file until you finish this project, and then submit this file as directed by your instructor.

9 **Close** ☒ the **Snipping Tool** window. **Close** ☒ WordPad, and then click **Don't Save**.

10 ▶ Display the **Start screen**, type **word 2013** and then open **Microsoft Word**. Compare your screen with Figure 1.44.

The Word program window has features that are common to other programs you have opened; for example, commands are arranged on tabs. When you create and save data in Word, you create a Word document file.

FIGURE 1.44

11 ▶ On the left, click **Open Other Documents**. Under **Open**, click **Computer**, and then click **Browse** to display the **Open** dialog box. Compare your screen with Figure 1.45, and then take a moment to study the table in Figure 1.46.

Recall that a dialog box is a window containing options for completing a task; its layout is similar to that of a File Explorer window. When you are working in a desktop app, use the Open dialog box to locate and open existing files that were created in the desktop app.

By default, the Open dialog box displays the path to the *Documents* folder of the user signed in. On your own computer, you can create a folder structure within the Documents folder to store your documents. Alternatively, you can use the skills you have practiced to navigate to other locations on your computer, such as your removable USB flash drive.

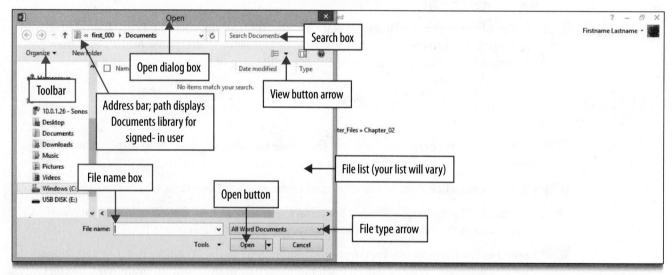

FIGURE 1.45

FIGURE 1.46

DIALOG BOX ELEMENT	FUNCTION
Address bar	Displays the path in the folder structure; by default, the path displays the Documents folder for the signed-in user.
File list	Displays the list of files and folders that are available in the folder indicated in the address bar.
File name box	Enables you to type the name of a specific file to locate it.
File type arrow	Enables you to restrict the type of files displayed in the file list; for example, the default *All Word Documents* restricts the type of files displayed to only Word documents. You can click the arrow and adjust the restrictions to a narrower or wider group of files.
Navigation pane	Enables access to Favorites, OneDrive, and This PC.
Search box	Filters the file list based on text that you type; the search is based on text in the file name and in the file itself, and on other properties that you can specify. The search takes place in the current folder, as displayed in the address bar, and in any subfolders within that folder.
Toolbar	Displays relevant tasks; for example, creating a new folder.

12 In the **navigation pane**, scroll down as necessary, and then under **This PC**, click your **USB flash drive**. In the **file list**, double-click the **Bell_Orchid** folder to open it and display its contents. In the upper right portion of the **Open** dialog box, click the **Change your view arrow** ⊞▾, and then set the view to **Large icons**. Compare your screen with Figure 1.47.

Notice that the Live Icons feature indicates that each folder contains additional subfolders.

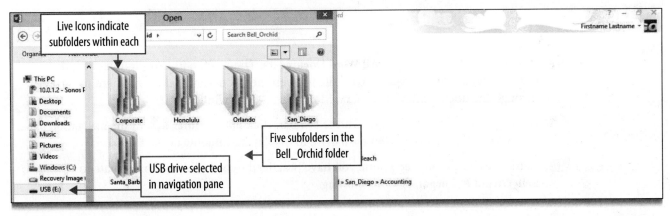

FIGURE 1.47

13 In the **file list**, double-click the **Corporate** folder, and then double-click the **Accounting** folder.

The view returns to the Details view.

14 In the **file list**, notice that only one document—a Word document—displays. In the lower right corner, notice that *All Word Documents* displays as the file type; this is the **File type** button. Click the **File type arrow**, and then on the displayed list, click **All Files**. Compare your screen with Figure 1.48.

When you change the file type to *All Files*, you can see that the Word file is not the only file in this folder. By default, the Open dialog box displays only the files created in the *active program*; however, you can display variations of file types in this manner.

Microsoft Office file types are identified by small icons, which is a convenient way to differentiate one type of file from another. Although you can view all the files in the folder, you can open only the files that were created in the active program, which in this instance is Microsoft Word.

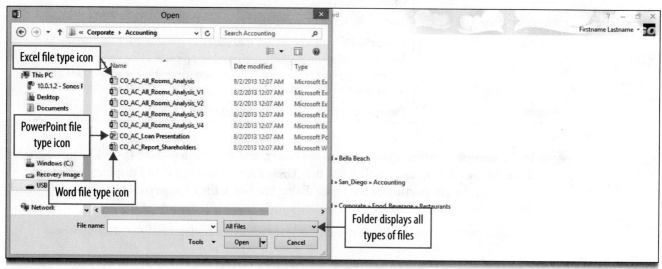

FIGURE 1.48

15 Change the file type back to **All Word Documents**. Then in the **file list**, double-click the **CO_AC_Report_Shareholders** Word file to open the document. Take a moment to scroll through the document. If necessary, Maximize ☐ the window.

16 Close ☒ the Word window. On the taskbar, click **File Explorer** ☐. In the **navigation pane**, under **This PC**, click your **USB flash drive** to display its contents in the **file list**.

17 In the **file list**, use any technique you have practiced to open folders to navigate to **Bell_Orchid** ▶ **Corporate** ▶ **Accounting**.

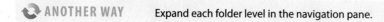

🔄 ANOTHER WAY   Expand each folder level in the navigation pane.

18 In the **file list**, double-click the **CO_AC_Loan_Presentation** file. When the **PowerPoint** window displays (a message regarding comments may display), if necessary Maximize ☐ the program window. Compare your screen with Figure 1.49.

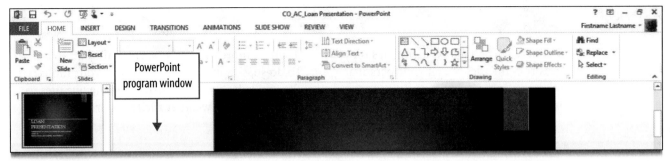

FIGURE 1.49

19 Close [×] the PowerPoint window.

20 In the **address bar**, to the right of **Bell_Orchid**, click ▶ and then compare your screen with Figure 1.50.

> Recall that the address bar is not just a path; rather, it contains active links from which you can click a folder name in the path, and then navigate directly to any displayed subfolders.

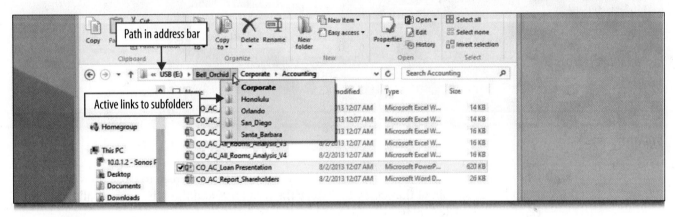

FIGURE 1.50

21 On the displayed list, click **Honolulu** to display the contents of the **Honolulu** folder in the **file list**. Open the **Food_Beverage** folder, and then open the **HO_FB_Banquet_Contract** file. Take a moment to view this document in the open Word program. **Close** [×] Word, and then **Close** [×] the **Food_Beverage** window.

More **Knowledge**	**Storing Files and Creating Desktop Shortcuts for a Program on Your Desktop**

On your desktop, you can add or remove *desktop shortcuts*, which are desktop icons that can link to items accessible on your computer such as a program, file, folder, disk drive, printer, or another computer. In previous versions of Windows, many computer users commonly did this.

Now the Start screen is your personal dashboard for all your programs and online activities, and increasingly you will access programs and your own files in the cloud. So do not clutter your desktop with shortcuts—doing so is more confusing than useful. Placing desktop shortcuts for frequently used programs or folders directly on your desktop may seem convenient, but as you add more icons, your desktop becomes cluttered and the shortcuts are not easy to find. A better organizing method is to use the taskbar for shortcuts to programs. For folders and files, the best organizing structure is to create a logical structure of folders within your Documents folder.

You can also drag frequently-used folders to the Favorites area in the navigation pane so that they are available any time you open File Explorer. As you progress in your use of Windows 8.1, you will discover techniques for using the taskbar and the Favorites area of the navigation pane to streamline your work, instead of cluttering your desktop.

Because you will use some tiles on your Start screen more than others, you will want to reposition the tiles to suit your personal needs. To do so, simply drag the tiles with your mouse or with your finger if you are using a touch device. You will also want to personalize the live tiles to display the information you want. For example, you can set the weather tile for your location.

Activity 1.15 | Personalizing Your Windows 8.1 Start Screen

1 Display the **Start screen**, and then type **file explorer** Point to the **File Explorer** app name that is shaded, and then right-click. Compare your screen with Figure 1.51.

From this menu, you can pin the app to the Start screen or to the taskbar on the desktop—or unpin from either of these locations.

FIGURE 1.51

2 Click **Pin to Start**, and then click on an empty area of the **Start screen** to close the search pane. Point to the bottom of the screen to display the scroll bar, and then drag the scroll bar to the right until the **File Explorer** tile comes into view as shown in Figure 1.52.

FIGURE 1.52

 BY TOUCH   Drag your finger to the left to scroll to the right.

3 Drag the **File Explorer** tile to the top of the first column of tiles on your **Start screen**, and then drag the **Desktop** tile under it.

With this tile, you can easily go directly to File Explorer from your Start screen.

4 Click the **Weather** tile, and, if necessary, follow the prompts to set the app to your location. Then, point to the upper right corner of the screen to display the title bar for the Weather app, and click **Close** ☒.

5 Display the **Start screen**, type **store** and press Enter to go the Windows Store. In the upper right, click in the search box, type **facebook** and then if you want to do so, install the Facebook app so that you can view your Facebook feed from your Start screen.

To see a tile for a newly-installed app, after an app is installed, search for it, and then pin it to your Start screen.

6 ▶ **Close** ❌ the Store app, redisplay your **Start screen**, point to the empty area below the first column of tiles to display an arrow, and then click the **arrow** to display the All apps view.

> Here you can view a small tile for every app—both desktop and Windows Store—in alphabetic order by category, by date installed, by name, or by most used depending on how you have set the All apps view.

7 ▶ **Press** ⊞ to redisplay the **Start screen** in the normal tiles view. Point to the extreme lower right corner of your screen, and then click **Minimize** ➖ to shrink the display of tiles.

> This view enables you see all of your tiles on one screen and is convenient for creating or moving groups.

8 ▶ **Click** any empty area of the screen to return to the normal view.

ALERT! **Allow Time to Complete the Remainder of This Project in One Session**

If you are working on a computer that is not your own, for example in a college lab, plan your time to complete the remainder of this project in one working session. Because you will need to store and then delete files on the hard disk drive of the computer at which you are working, it is recommended that you complete the remainder of this project in one working session—*unless you are working on your own computer or you know that the files will be retained.* In your college lab, it is possible that files you store on the computer's hard drive will not be retained after you sign off. Allow approximately 25 to 40 minutes for the remainder of this project.

Objective 9   Create, Rename, and Copy Files and Folders

File management includes organizing, copying, naming, renaming, moving, and deleting the files and folders you have stored in various locations—both locally and in the cloud.

Activity 1.16 | Copying Files from a Removable Storage Device to the Documents Folder on the Hard Disk Drive

Barbara and Steven have the assignment to transfer and then organize some of the corporation's files to a computer that will be connected to the corporate network. Data on such a computer can be accessed by employees at any of the hotel locations through the use of sharing technologies. For example, *SharePoint* is a Microsoft technology that enables employees in an organization to access information across organizational and geographic boundaries.

1 ▶ On the Windows 8.1 **Start screen**, click the **Desktop tile** to display your Windows 8.1 desktop. If necessary, insert the USB flash drive that contains the student data files that accompany this chapter that you downloaded from the Pearson website or obtained from your instructor. Open **File Explorer** 📁 and display the window for your USB flash drive.

> Recall that in the This PC window, you have access to all the storage areas inside your computer, such as your hard disk drives, and to any devices with removable storage, such as CDs, DVDs, or USB flash drives.

2 ▶ In the **file list**, click **Bell_Orchid** to select the folder. Compare your screen with Figure 1.53.

FIGURE 1.53

3 With the **Bell_Orchid** folder on your USB drive selected, on the ribbon, on the **Home tab**, in the **Clipboard group**, click **Copy**.

4 To the left of the **address bar**, click the **Up** button ⬆ one time. In the **file list**, double-click your **Documents** folder to open it, and then on the **Home tab**, in the **Clipboard group**, click **Paste**.

A progress bar displays in the dialog box, and also displays on the File Explorer taskbar button with green shading. A progress bar indicates visually the progress of a task such as a copy process, a download, or a file transfer.

The Documents folder is one of several folders within your *personal folder* stored on the hard disk drive. For each user account—even if there is only one user on the computer—Windows 8.1 creates a personal folder labeled with the account holder's name.

> **NOTE** **The *Copy to* Command on the Ribbon**
>
> If you click the *Copy to* command in the Organize group, and then click Documents, the selected file or folder is copied to your OneDrive Documents folder. To use this command to copy to other locations, at the bottom click Choose location, and then navigate to the location to which you want to copy.

5 In your **Documents** folder, point to the selected **Bell_Orchid** folder, hold down the left mouse button, drag the folder down to the taskbar until the ScreenTip *Pin to File Explorer* displays, and then release the left mouse button. Notice that the **Jump List** for **File Explorer** displays and that the **Bell_Orchid** folder in your **Documents** folder is pinned to the top of it.

By pinning the folder to the Jump List, you will be able to access it quickly. You can point to the pinned folder to see its path in the Documents folder.

6 Click anywhere on the desktop to close the Jump List, and then, **Close** ❌ the **Documents** window.

Activity 1.17 | Creating and Renaming Folders

Barbara and Steven can see that various managers have been placing files related to the new European hotels in the *Future_Hotels* folder. They can also see that the files have not been organized into a logical structure. For example, files that are related to each other are not in separate folders; instead they are mixed in with other files that are not related to the topic.

In this activity, you will create, name, and rename folders to begin a logical structure of folders in which to organize the files related to the European hotels project.

1 On the taskbar, right-click the **File Explorer** button 🗂 to display the **Jump List**, and then under **Pinned**, click **Bell_Orchid**.

2 In the **address bar**, to the right of **Bell_Orchid**, click ▶, and then on the list click **Corporate**. To the right of **Corporate**, click ▶, and then click **Information_Technology**. To the right of **Information_Technology**, click ▶, and then click **Future_Hotels**.

Some computer users prefer to navigate a folder structure using the address bar in this manner. Use whichever method you prefer—double-clicking in the file list, or clicking in the address bar.

↻ ANOTHER WAY   In the file list, double-click the Corporate folder, double-click the Information_Technology folder, and then double-click the Future_Hotels folder to display its contents in the file list. Or, in the navigation pane, click Documents, and expand each folder in the navigation pane.

3 Be sure the items are in alphabetical order by **Name**. If the items are not in alphabetical order, recall that by clicking on the column heading name, you can change how the files in the file list are ordered. On the ribbon, click the **View tab**, and then in the **Layout group**, be sure **Details** is selected. If necessary, set the view to Details.

The *Details view* displays a list of files or folders and their most common properties.

↻ ANOTHER WAY   Right-click in a blank area of the file list, point to View, and then click Details.

4 On the ribbon, click the **Home tab**, and then in the **New group**, click **New folder**. With the text *New folder* selected, type **Paris** and press ⏎. Click **New folder** again, and then type **Venice** and press ⏎.

5 Create a new folder named **Essex** and press ⏎. Click the **Venice** folder, and then on the ribbon, in the **Organize group**, click **Rename**. Notice that the text *Venice* is selected. Type **Rome** and press ⏎.

↻ ANOTHER WAY   Point to a folder or file name, right-click, and then on the shortcut menu, click Rename.

6 Click the **Essex** folder one time to select it. Point to the selected **Essex** folder, and then click one time again. With the text selected, type **London** and press ⏎ to change the folder name.

You can use either of these techniques to change the name of a folder.

7 From the taskbar, start **Snipping Tool**; if necessary drag the *title bar*—the bar across the top of a window that displays the program name—of Snipping Tool into a blank area of the desktop. Click the **New arrow**, and then click **Window Snip**. Point anywhere in the **Future_Hotels** window and click one time. In the **Snipping Tool** mark-up window, click **Save Snip** 💾.

8 In the **Save As** dialog box, in the **navigation pane**, scroll down as necessary, and then click your **USB flash drive** so that it displays in the **address bar**.

9 In the **file list**, double-click your **Windows 8.1 Projects** folder to open it. Click in the **File name** box, and then replace the selected text by typing **Lastname_Firstname_1B_Europe_Folders_Snip**

10 Be sure the file type is **JPEG**. Click **Save** or press ⏎. **Close** ❌ the **Snipping Tool** window. Hold this file until you finish this Project. Leave the **Future_Hotels** window open.

Activity 1.18 | Renaming Files

1 In the **address bar**, click **Information_Technology** to move up one level in the folder structure—or click the Up button ⬆.

2 On the ribbon, click the **View tab**, and then in the **Current view group**, click **Size all columns to fit** ⊞ to make it easier to see all the information about the files and folders.

3 Using any of the techniques you practiced to rename a folder, rename the **Dogs** file as **Dogs_1** Rename the **MoreDogs** file to **Dogs_2** and then compare your screen with Figure 1.54.

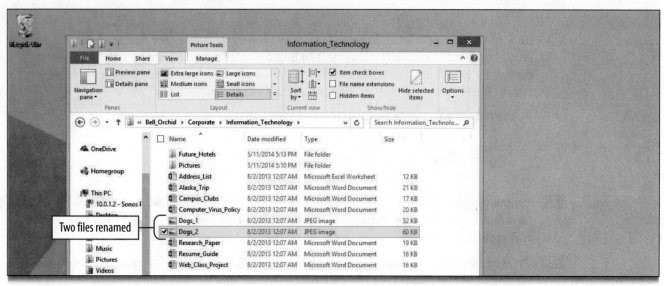

FIGURE 1.54

4 Close ❌ the **Information_Technology** window.

Activity 1.19 | Copying Files

Copying, moving, renaming, and deleting files and folders comprise the most heavily used features within File Explorer. Probably half or more of the steps you complete in File Explorer relate to these tasks, so mastering these techniques will increase your efficiency.

When you *copy* a file or a folder, you make a duplicate of the original item and then store the duplicate in another location. In this activity, you will assist Barbara and Steven in making copies of the Staffing_Plan file, and then placing the copies in each of the three folders you created— London, Paris, and Rome.

1 In the taskbar, point to the **File Explorer** button 📁, hold down the left mouse button, and then drag upward slightly into the desktop to display the **Jump List**. Then, on the **Jump List**, under **Pinned**, click **Bell_Orchid**.

You will increase your efficiency if you make it a habit to work mostly from the taskbar and to display Jump Lists using this technique. After the Jump List displays, you need only move your mouse pointer upward a little more to select the action that you want.

🔁 **BY TOUCH**   Swipe upward with a quick short gesture to display the Jump List.

2 With the **Bell_Orchid** window displayed, by double-clicking in the file list or following the links in the address bar, navigate to **Corporate ▶ Information_Technology ▶ Future_Hotels**.

3 **Maximize** ☐ the window. On the **View tab**, if necessary set the **Layout** to **Details**, and then in the **Current view group**, click **Size all columns to fit**.

4 In the **file list**, click the file **Staffing_Plan** one time to select it, and then on the **Home tab**, in the **Clipboard group**, click **Copy**.

> The Copy command places a copy of your selected file or folder on the *Clipboard* where it will be stored until you use the Paste command to insert the copy somewhere else. The Clipboard is a temporary storage area for information that you have copied or moved from one place and plan to use somewhere else.
>
> In Windows 8.1, the Clipboard can hold only one piece of information at a time. Whenever something is copied to the Clipboard, it replaces whatever was there before. In Windows 8.1, you cannot view the contents of the Clipboard nor place multiple items there in the manner that you can in Microsoft Word.

5 At the top of the **file list**, double-click the **London folder** to open it, and then on the ribbon, in the **Clipboard group**, click **Paste**. Notice that the copy of the **Staffing_Plan** file displays. Compare your screen with Figure 1.55.

FIGURE 1.55

 **ANOTHER WAY**   Right-click the file you want to copy, and then on the menu click Copy. Then right-click the folder into which you want to place the copy, and on the menu click Paste. Or, select the file you want to copy, press Ctrl + C to activate the Copy command, open the folder into which you want to paste the file, and then press Ctrl + V to activate the Paste command.

6 With the **London** window open, by using any of the techniques you have practiced, rename this copy of the **Staffing_Plan** file to **London_Staffing_Plan**

7 In the **address bar**, click **Future_Hotels** to redisplay this window and move up one level in the folder structure.

8 Click the **Staffing_Plan** file one time to select it, hold down Ctrl, and then drag the file upward over the **Paris** folder until the ScreenTip + *Copy to Paris* displays as shown in Figure 1.56, and then release the mouse button and release Ctrl.

> When dragging a file into a folder, holding down Ctrl engages the Copy command and places a *copy* of the file at the location where you release the mouse button. This is another way to copy a file or copy a folder.

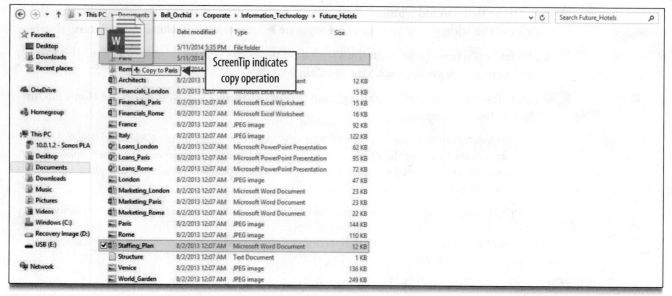

FIGURE 1.56

9 ▶ Open the **Paris** folder, and then rename the **Staffing_Plan** file **Paris_Staffing_Plan** Then, move up one level in the folder structure to display the **Future_Hotels** window.

10 ▶ Using either of the techniques you have practiced, copy the **Staffing_Plan** file to the **Rome** folder.

11 ▶ In the **Rome** folder, rename the file **Rome_Staffing_Plan**

12 ▶ On the **address bar**, click **Future_Hotels** to move up one level and open the **Future_Hotels** window—or click the Up button ⬆ to move up one level. Leave this folder open for the next activity.

Objective 10 Move and Delete Files and Folders

When you *move* a file or folder, you remove it from the original location and store it in a new location. To keep your computer organized, delete files you no longer need.

Activity 1.20 | Moving Files

In this activity, you will move items from the Future_Hotels folder into their appropriate folders.

1 ▶ With the **Future_Hotels** folder open, in the **file list**, click the Excel file **Financials_London** one time to select it. On the **Home tab**, in the **Clipboard group**, click **Cut**.

The file's Excel icon dims. This action places the item on the Clipboard.

🔄 **ANOTHER WAY**   Right-click the file or folder, and on the shortcut menu, click Cut; or, select the file or folder, and then press Ctrl + X .

2 ▶ Double-click the **London** folder to open it, and then on the **Home tab**, in the **Clipboard group**, click **Paste**.

🔄 **ANOTHER WAY**   Right-click the folder, and on the shortcut menu, click Paste; or, select the folder, and then press Ctrl + V .

3 On the **address bar**, click **Future_Hotels** to move up a level. In the **file list**, point to **Financials_Paris**, hold down the left mouse button, and then drag the file upward over the **Paris** folder until the ScreenTip → *Move to Paris* displays, and then release the mouse button.

4 Open the **Paris** folder, and notice that the file was moved to this folder. On the **address bar**, click **Future_Hotels** to return to that folder.

5 Using either of the techniques you just practiced, move the **Financials_Rome** file into the **Rome** folder.

6 Hold down Ctrl, and then in the file list, click **Loans_London**, **London**, and **Marketing_London** to select the three files. Release the Ctrl key. Compare your screen with Figure 1.57.

Use this technique to select a group of noncontiguous items in a list.

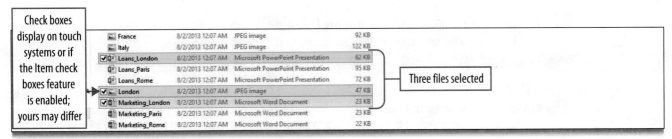

FIGURE 1.57

7 Point to any of the selected files, hold down the left mouse button, and then drag upward over the **London** folder until the ScreenTip → *Move to London* displays and 3 displays over the files being moved, and then release the mouse button.

> **ANOTHER WAY**   Right-click over any of the selected files, click Cut, right-click over the London folder, and then click Paste.

8 Using either the select and drag method, or the select and then Cut and Paste method, select the files **France**, **Loans_Paris**, **Marketing_Paris**, and **Paris**, and move these four files into the **Paris** folder.

9 Select the four files **Italy**, **Loans_Rome**, **Marketing_Rome**, and **Rome**, and move them into the **Rome** folder.

You can see that by keeping related files together, for example, all the files that relate to the Rome hotel, in folders that have an appropriately descriptive name, it will be easier to locate information later.

> **ANOTHER WAY**   If a group of files to be selected are contiguous (next to each other in the file list), click the first file to be selected, hold down Shift, and then click the last file to select all of the files between the top and bottom file selections.

10 Move the **Architects** file into the **London** folder.

11 In an empty area of the file list, right-click, and then click **Undo Move**. Leave the **Future_Hotels** window open for the next activity.

Any action that you make in a file list can be undone in this manner.

> **ANOTHER WAY**   Press Ctrl + Z to undo an action in the file list.

Activity 1.21 | Copying and Moving Files by Snapping Two Windows

Sometimes you will want to open, in a second window, another instance of a program that you are using; that is, two copies of the program will be running simultaneously. This capability is especially useful in the File Explorer program, because you are frequently moving or copying files from one location to another.

In this activity, you will open two instances of File Explorer, and then use the *Snap* feature to display both instances on your screen.

To copy or move files or folders into a different level of a folder structure, or to a different drive location, the most efficient method is to display two windows side by side and then use drag and drop or copy (or cut) and paste commands.

In this activity, you will assist Barbara and Steven in making copies of the Staffing_Plan files for the corporate office.

1 In the upper right corner, click **Restore Down** 🗗 to restore the **Future_Hotels** window to its previous size and not maximized on the screen.

2 Hold down 🪟 and press ← to snap the window so that it occupies the left half of the screen.

3 On the taskbar, drag the **File Explorer** button 📁 upward slightly into the desktop to display the **Jump List**, and then click **Bell_Orchid** to open a new window. Hold down 🪟 and press → to snap this window to the right side of the screen.

4 In the window on the right, navigate to **Corporate ▶ Human_Resources**. Compare your screen with Figure 1.58.

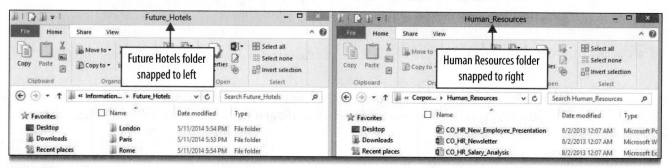

FIGURE 1.58

 **ANOTHER WAY**

Drag the title bar of a window to the left or right side of the screen to snap it into place. Remember to position your mouse so that you have enough space to drag it on your desk surface to the left or to the right about 6 inches. Then, point to the upper edge of the window and drag the window to the left or right until the pointer reaches the edge of the screen and the window snaps into place and occupies half of the screen.

5 In the left window, open the **Rome** folder, and then select the file **Rome_Staffing_Plan**.

6 Hold down Ctrl, and then drag the file into the right window, into an empty area of the **Human_Resources file list**, until the ScreenTip + *Copy to Human_Resources* displays, and then release the mouse button and the Ctrl key.

7 In the left window, on the **address bar**, click **Future_Hotels** to redisplay that folder. Open the **Paris** folder, point to **Paris_Staffing_Plan** and right-click, and then click **Copy**.

8 In the right window, point anywhere in the **file list**, right-click, and then click **Paste**.

9 Navigate to the **London** folder, and then use either technique to copy the **London_Staffing_Plan** file on the left to the folder on the right.

Copies of the three files regarding staffing plans for the three European locations display.

10 Start the **Snipping Tool** program, click the **New arrow**, and then click **Full-screen Snip**. In the **Snipping Tool** mark-up window, click **Save Snip** 🖫.

11 In the displayed **Save As** dialog box, notice the path in the **address bar**. If necessary, in the navigation pane, under **This PC**, click your USB flash drive, and then display the window for your **Windows 8.1 Projects** folder.

12 Be sure the file type is **JPEG**. Using your own name, name the file **Lastname_Firstname_1B_HR_Snip** and press Enter.

13 **Close** ⬛ all open windows. As directed by your instructor, submit the three files that are the results of this project.

More Knowledge **Using the Recycle Bin Icon, Permanently Deleting an Item, and Restoring by Dragging**

It is good practice to delete files and folders that you no longer need from your hard disk drive and removable storage devices. Doing so frees up storage space on your devices and makes it easier to keep your data organized.

When you delete a file or folder from any area of your computer's hard disk drive, the file or folder is not immediately deleted. Instead, the deleted item is stored in the *Recycle Bin* and remains there until the Recycle Bin is emptied. Thus, you can recover an item deleted from your computer's hard disk drive so long as the Recycle Bin has not been emptied. Items deleted from removable storage devices like a USB flash drive and from some network drives are immediately deleted and cannot be recovered from the Recycle Bin.

To permanently delete a file without first moving it to the Recycle Bin, click the item, hold down Shift, and then press Delete. A message will display indicating *Are you sure you want to permanently delete this file?* Use caution when using Shift + Delete to permanently delete a file because this action is *not* reversible.

You can restore items by dragging them from the file list of the Recycle Bin window to the file list of the folder window in which you want to restore or you can restore them to the location they were deleted from by right-clicking the items in the file list of the Recycle Bin window and selecting Restore.

END | You have completed Project 1B

END OF CHAPTER

SUMMARY

Windows 8.1 is optimized for touchscreens and also works with a mouse and keyboard. You will probably use touch when you are reading or communicating on the web and a keyboard when creating files.

The Windows 8.1 Start screen is your connected dashboard—this is your one-screen view of information that updates continuously with new information and personal communications that are important to you.

The Windows Store apps you use from the Start screen are immersive—they have no borders or screen distractions. Windows Store apps typically have a single purpose; for example, to view Facebook updates.

File Explorer is at work anytime you are viewing the contents of a location, a folder, or a file. Use File Explorer to navigate your Windows 8.1 structure that stores and organizes the files you create.

GO! LEARN IT ONLINE

Review the concepts and key terms in this chapter by completing these online challenges, which you can find at **www.pearsonhighered.com/go** or in MyITLab.

Matching and Multiple Choice: Answer matching and multiple choice questions to test what you learned in this chapter. MyITLab

Crossword Puzzle: Spell out the words that match the numbered cues, and put them in the puzzle squares.

GO! FOR JOB SUCCESS

Video: Email Etiquette

Your instructor may assign this video to your class, and then ask you to think about, or discuss with your classmates, these questions:

FotoIEdhar / Fotolia

Why do you think it is important to follow specific etiquette when composing email?

Why is it important to include a greeting and sign every email you send?

What are the differences between sending a business email and a personal email, and what are three specific things you should never do in a business email?

END OF CHAPTER

REVIEW AND ASSESSMENT GUIDE FOR WINDOWS 8.1 CHAPTER 1

Your instructor may assign one or more of these projects to help you review the chapter and assess your mastery and understanding of the chapter.

	REVIEW AND ASSESSMENT GUIDE FOR WINDOWS 8.1 CHAPTER 1		
PROJECT	**APPLY SKILLS FROM THESE CHAPTER OBJECTIVES**	**PROJECT TYPE**	**PROJECT LOCATION**
1C	Objectives 1–5 from Project 1A	**1C Skills Review** A guided review of the skills from Project 1A.	On the following pages
1D	Objectives 6–10 from Project 1B	**1D Skills Review** A guided review of the skills from Project 1B.	On the following pages
1E	Objectives 1–5 from Project 1A	**1E Mastering** A demonstration of your mastery of the skills in Project 1A with decision making.	On the following pages
1F	Objectives 6–10 from Project 1B	**1F Mastering** A demonstration of your mastery of the skills in Project 1B with decision making.	On the following pages
1G	Combination of Objectives from Projects 1A and 1B	**1G GO! Think** A demonstration of your understanding of the chapter concepts applied in a manner that you would outside of college. An analytic rubric helps you and your instructor grade the quality of your work by comparing it to the work an expert in the discipline would create.	On the following pages
1H	Combination of Objectives from Projects 1A and 1B	**1H GO! Think** A demonstration of your understanding of the chapter concepts applied in a manner that you would outside of college. An analytic rubric helps you and your instructor grade the quality of your work by comparing it to the work an expert in the discipline would create.	On the following pages
1I	Combination of Objectives from Projects 1A and 1B	**1I GO! Think** A demonstration of your understanding of the chapter concepts applied in a manner that you would outside of college. An analytic rubric helps you and your instructor grade the quality of your work by comparing it to the work an expert in the discipline would create.	On the following pages

GLOSSARY

GLOSSARY OF CHAPTER KEY TERMS

.jpg: An image file format, commonly pronounced *JPEG*, that stands for Joint Photographic Experts Group; this is a common file type used by digital cameras and computers to store digital pictures; JPEG is popular because it can store a high-quality picture in a relatively small file.

.png: An image file format, commonly pronounced *PING*, that stands for Portable Network Graphic; this is an image file type that can be transferred over the Internet.

Action Center: Located in the notification area, a central place to view alerts and take actions related to things that need your attention.

Address bar: Displays your current location in the folder structure as a series of links separated by arrows.

Administrator account: A user account that lets you make changes that will affect other users of the computer; the most powerful of the account types, because it permits the most control over the computer.

App: The shortened version of the word *application*.

App bar: An area at the top or bottom of every Windows Store app containing various controls pertaining to the app.

Apps view: The Start screen view in which all apps have the same small tile size and the apps cans be arranged in various ways.

Application: A set of instructions that a computer uses to accomplish a task; also called a program.

Badge: An icon that displays on the lock screen, below the time, day, and date, that represents the status of your Internet connection, your battery if you are using a tablet or laptop, or any other lock screen apps you might have selected.

Booting the computer: The process of turning on a computer when the computer has been completely shut down.

Charms: A set of buttons that display when you point or swipe in from the right side of the screen that you can use in every app—whether a Windows Store app or a desktop app—and that enables you to search, share, access devices, or adjust your PC settings.

Click: The action of pressing the left mouse button.

Clipboard: A temporary storage area for information that you have copied or moved from one place and plan to use somewhere else.

Cloud storage: Storage space on an Internet site that can also display as a drive on your computer.

Compressed file: A file that has been reduced in size and that takes up less storage space and can be transferred to other computers faster than uncompressed files.

Contextual tab: Context-sensitive commands and options on the ribbon that are relevant to the active object.

Dashboard: A descriptive term for the Windows 8.1 Start screen because it provides a one-screen view of links to information and programs that matter most to the signed-in user.

Data: All the files—documents, workbooks, pictures, songs, and so on—that you create and store during the day-to-day use of your computer.

Data management: The process of managing your files and folders in an organized manner so that you can find information when you need it.

Desktop: The area in Windows 8.1 where you use desktop apps and that serves as a surface for your work, like the top of an actual desk.

Desktop app: A computer program installed on the hard drive of a computer and that requires a computer operating system like Microsoft Windows or Apple OS to run.

Desktop background: Displays the colors and graphics of your desktop; you can change the desktop background to look the way you want it.

Desktop shortcuts: Desktop icons that link to any item accessible on your computer or on a network, such as a program, file, folder, disk drive, printer, or another computer.

Details pane: Displays the most common properties associated with the selected file.

Details view: The file list view in File Explorer that displays a list of files or folders and their most common properties.

Dialog box: A small window that displays options for completing a task.

Double-click: The action of pressing the left mouse button twice in rapid succession while holding the mouse still.

Drag: The action of moving something from one location on the screen to another while holding down the left mouse button; the action of dragging includes releasing the mouse button at the desired time or location.

Drive: An area of storage that is formatted with a file system compatible with your operating system and is identified by a drive letter.

Extract: The action of decompressing—pulling out—files from a compressed form.

File: A collection of information that is stored on a computer under a single name, for example a text document, a picture, or a program.

File Explorer: The program within Windows 8.1 that displays the contents of folders and files on your computer, and which also enables you to perform tasks related to your files and folders such as copying, moving, and renaming. File Explorer is at work anytime you are viewing the contents of a folder or a file.

File Explorer window: Displays the contents of the current folder or device and contains helpful parts so that you can navigate—explore within the organizing structure of Windows.

File list: Displays the contents of the current folder; if you type text into the Search box, only the folders and files that match your search will display here—including files in subfolders.

File properties: Information about a file such as its author, the date the file was last changed, and any descriptive tags.

Folder: A container in which you store files.

Folder structure: The hierarchy of folders in Windows 8.1.

Free-form snip: When using Snipping Tool, the type of snip that lets you draw an irregular line, such as a circle, around an area of the screen.

Full-screen snip: When using Snipping Tool, the type of snip that captures the entire screen.

Graphical user interface: The system by which you interact with your computer and which uses graphics such as an image of a file folder or wastebasket that you click to activate the item represented.

GUI: The acronym for a graphical user interface, pronounced *GOO-ee*.

Hard disk drive: The primary storage device located inside your computer and where most of your files and programs are typically stored; usually labeled as drive C.

Hierarchy: An arrangement where items are ranked and where each level is lower in rank than the item above it.

Icons: Small images that represent commands, files, applications, or other windows.

Immersive: The term that describes the Windows 8.1 style screens, meaning they have no borders, no menus, and they behave differently from traditional Windows desktop programs because there is no taskbar; the idea is that you are immersed in the app with no screen distractions.

Insertion point: A blinking vertical line that indicates where text or graphics will be inserted.

Internet Explorer: The web browser program developed by Microsoft that is included with Windows 8.1.

JPEG: An acronym for Joint Photographic Experts Group, and which is a common file type used by digital cameras and computers to store digital pictures; JPEG is popular because it can store a high-quality picture in a relatively small file. A JPEG file has a .jpg file extension.

Jump List: A list that displays when you right-click a button on the taskbar, and which displays locations (in the upper portion) and tasks (in the lower portion) from a program's taskbar button.

Keyboard shortcut: A combination of two or more keyboard keys, used to perform a task that would otherwise require a mouse.

Left pane: The pane on the left side of a File Explorer window.

Live tiles: Tiles on the Windows 8.1 Start screen that are constantly updated with fresh information relevant to the signed-in user; for example, the number of new email messages, new sports scores of interest, or new updates to social networks such as Facebook or Twitter.

Local account: A user account in which the information associated with each user is local to a single Windows 8.1 computer.

Location: Any disk drive, folder, or other place in which you can store files and folders.

Lock screen: The first screen that displays after turning on a Windows 8.1 device, which displays the time, day, and date, and one or more icons representing the status of the device's Internet connection, battery status on a tablet or laptop, and any lock screen apps that are installed such as email notifications.

Lock screen apps: Apps that display on a Windows 8.1 lock screen and that show quick status and notifications, even if the screen is locked, and include Calendar, Mail, Messaging, and Weather.

Menu: A list of commands within a category.

Menu bar: A group of menus.

Microsoft account: A user account that allows you to set up one Windows 8.1 computer and then synchronize all the same settings from that computer to any other device you have that uses Windows 8.1.

Modern design: The design principles in Windows 8.1 that include tiles with white text on deeply colored backgrounds, consistent fonts, simpler navigation, and the use of the entire screen; the idea is that you are immersed in the app with no screen distractions.

Mouse pointer: Any symbol that displays on your screen in response to moving your mouse.

Navigate (File Explorer): Explore within the file organizing structure of Windows 8.1.

Navigation pane: The area on the left side of a File Explorer window; it displays favorites, network locations, and an expandable list of drives and folders.

Notification area: Displays notification icons and the system clock; sometimes referred to as the *system tray*.

Notification bar: In Internet Explorer 11, a bar at the bottom of your screen that displays information about pending downloads, security issues, add-ons, and other issues related to the operation of your computer.

OneDrive: A free file storage and file sharing service provided by Microsoft when you sign up for a Microsoft account.

Operating system: A specific type of computer program that manages the other programs on a computer—including computer devices such as desktop computers, laptop computers, smartphones, tablet computers, and game consoles.

Paint: A program that comes with Windows 8.1 with which you can create and edit drawings and display and edit stored photos.

Parent folder: In the file organizing structure of File Explorer, the location where the folder you are viewing is saved—one level up in the hierarchy.

Path: A sequence of folders (directories) that leads to a specific file or folder.

PC settings: The area from which you can control almost everything about how Windows 8.1 looks and works; you can change colors and backgrounds, the picture on your lock screen or account picture, manage other users (if you are the administrator), connect devices like printers, or set up a network.

Personal folder: A folder created for each user account on a Windows 8.1 computer, labeled with the account holder's name, and which contains the subfolders *Documents, Pictures, Music,* and *Videos.*

PING: An acronym for Portable Network Graphic, and which is a common file type that can be transferred over the Internet. A PING file has a .png file extension.

Point to: The action of moving the mouse pointer over a specific area.

Pointer: Any symbol that displays on your screen in response to moving your mouse and with which you can select objects and commands.

Pointing device: A mouse, touchpad, or other device that controls the pointer position on the screen.

Program: A set of instructions that a computer uses to accomplish a task; also called an application.

Progress bar: In a dialog box or taskbar button, a bar that indicates visually the progress of a task such as a download or file transfer.

Rectangular snip: When using Snipping Tool, the type of snip that lets you draw a precise box by dragging the mouse pointer around an area of the screen to form a rectangle.

Recycle Bin: A folder that stores anything that you delete from your computer, and from which anything stored can be retrieved until the contents are permanently deleted by activating the Empty Recycle Bin command.

Removable storage device: A portable device on which you can store files, such as a USB flash drive, a flash memory card, or an external hard drive, commonly used to transfer information from one computer to another.

Resources: A term used to refer collectively to the parts of your computer such as the central processing unit (CPU), memory, and any attached devices such as a printer.

Ribbon: The area at the top of a window in File Explorer that groups common tasks such as copying and moving, creating new folders, emailing and zipping items, and changing views on related tabs.

Right-click: The action of clicking the right mouse button.

Roam: The ability to set up one computer, for example a desktop computer, and then synchronize—roam—all the same settings to a laptop, to a tablet PC, to a Windows phone, or to any other device to which one signs in with the same Microsoft account.

Screen capture: An image file that contains the contents of a computer screen.

Screenshot: Another name for a screen capture.

ScreenTip: Useful information that displays in a small box on the screen when you perform various mouse actions, such as pointing to screen elements.

Scroll arrow: An arrow at the top and or bottom, or left and right, of a scroll bar that when clicked, moves the window in small increments.

Scroll bar: A bar that displays on the bottom or right side of a window when the contents of a window are not completely visible; used to move the window up, down, left, or right to bring the contents into view.

Scroll box: The box in a vertical or horizontal scroll bar that you drag to reposition the document on the screen.

Select: To specify, by highlighting, a block of data or text on the screen with the intent of performing some action on the selection.

SharePoint: A Microsoft technology that enables employees in an organization to access information across organizational and geographic boundaries.

Shortcut menu: A context-sensitive menu that displays commands and options relevant to the active object.

Shut down: Turning off your computer in a manner that closes all open programs and files, closes your network

connections, stops the hard disk, and discontinues the use of electrical power.

Sleep: Turning off your computer in a manner that automatically saves your work, stops the fan, and uses a small amount of electrical power to maintain your work in memory.

Snap (desktop apps): A Windows 8.1 desktop feature that automatically resizes windows when you move—*snap*—them to the edge of the screen.

Snip: The image captured using Snipping Tool.

Snipping Tool: A program included with Windows 8.1 with which you can capture an image of all or part of a computer screen, and then annotate, save, copy, or share the image via email.

Speakers icon: Displays the status of the computer's speakers (if any).

Split button: A button that has two parts—a button and an arrow; clicking the main part of the button performs a command and clicking the arrow opens a menu with choices.

Start screen: The first screen that displays after signing in to a Windows 8.1 device and that displays square and rectangular boxes—referred to as tiles—from which you can access apps, websites, programs, and tools for using the computer by clicking or tapping them.

System tray: Another name for the notification area on the taskbar.

Tags: Properties that you create and add to a file to help you find and organize your files.

Taskbar: The area of the desktop that contains program buttons, and buttons for all open programs; by default, it is located at the bottom of the desktop, but you can move it.

Thumbnail: A reduced image of a graphic.

Tiles: Square and rectangular boxes on the Windows 8.1 Start screen from which you can access apps, websites, programs, and tools for using the computer by simply clicking or tapping them.

Title bar: The bar across the top of the window that displays the program name.

User account: A collection of information that tells Windows 8.1 what files and folders the account holder can access, what changes the account holder can make to the computer system, and what the account holder's personal preferences are.

Wallpaper: Another term for the desktop background.

Web browser: Software with which you display webpages and navigate the Internet.

Window snip: When using Snipping Tool, the type of snip that captures the entire displayed window.

Windows 8.1: An operating system developed by Microsoft Corporation

designed to work with mobile computing devices of all types and also with traditional PCs.

Windows Store apps: Apps built for specific purposes; for example, to view photos, read sports information, organize a list of contacts, or read updates to social networks like Facebook and Twitter.

CHAPTER REVIEW

PROJECT FILES

Apply 1A skills from these Objectives:

1 Use File Explorer and Desktop Apps to Create a New Folder and Save a File on a Removable Storage Device

2 Identify the Functions of the Windows 8.1 Operating System and Windows Store Apps

3 Use Windows Store Apps

4 Sign Out of Windows 8.1 and Turn Off Your Computer

5 Customize and Manage User Accounts

For Project 1C, you will need the following files:

Your USB flash drive containing the student data files
Win81_1C_Answer_Sheet (Word document)

You will save your file as:

Lastname_Firstname_1C_Answer_Sheet

1 Display the **Start screen**; point to the upper left corner and drag down slightly to display any open apps; close any open apps. Display the **desktop**. **Close** ☒ any open desktop windows. On the taskbar, click **File Explorer**. In the **navigation pane**, click your **USB drive** that contains the student files for this chapter, and then navigate to **Chapter_Files ▶ Chapter_01**. Double-click the Word file **win81_1C_Answer_Sheet** to open Word and display the document. If necessary, at the top click Enable editing; be sure the window is maximized. In the upper left corner, click **FILE**, click **Save As**, click **Computer**, and then click **Browse** to display the **Save As** dialog box. In the **navigation pane**, click your **USB drive**, and then double-click to open your **Windows 8.1 Projects** folder. Using your own name, save the document as **Lastname_Firstname_1C_Answer_Sheet** Click **Save**.

On the taskbar, click the **Word** button to minimize the window and leave your Word document accessible from the taskbar. **Close** the **Chapter_01** window. As you complete each step in this project, write the letter of your answer on a piece of paper; you will fill in your Answer Sheet after you complete all the steps in this project.

Display the **Start screen** and type **paint** Which of the following is true?

A.   Search terms that begin with the text *paint* display in the search results.

B.   The Paint program opens on the desktop.

C.   From this screen, you can remove the Paint program from your computer.

2 Click the name of the *Paint* program. What is your result?

A.   The Paint program tile displays on the Start screen.

B.   The Paint program opens on the desktop.

C.   File Explorer displays files created in the Paint program.

3 On the taskbar, point to the **Paint** button, right-click, and then click **Pin this program to taskbar**. Then **Close** ☒ the **Paint** window. Which of the following is true?

A.   Both B. and C. are true.

B.   The Paint program closes.

C.   The Paint program button displays on the taskbar because it is pinned there.

4 On the taskbar, click **File Explorer**. What is your result?

A.   The window for your USB flash drive displays.

B.   The This PC window displays.

C.   The Documents window displays.

(Project 1C Exploring Windows 8.1 continues on the next page)

5 In the file list, double-click **Documents**. What is your result?

A. The first document in the folder opens in its application.

B. The contents of the Documents folder display in the file list.

C. The contents of the Documents folder display in the address bar.

6 In the **navigation pane**, click **This PC**. What is your result?

A. The storage devices attached to your computer display in the file list.

B. All of the files on the hard drive display in the file list.

C. Your computer restarts.

7 **Close** ☒ the **This PC** window. On the taskbar, point to the **Paint** button, right-click, and then click **Unpin this program from taskbar**. Display the **Start screen**. Type **store** and press ⏎. What is your result?

A. All **the s**torage devices attached to your computer display on the Start screen.

B. The Store app displays.

C. A list of games that you can download displays.

8 Display the **Start screen**, type **maps** and press ⏎; if necessary, enable your current location. Display the **Start screen** again, type **weather** and then press ⏎. Display the **Start screen** again, point to the upper left corner of the screen, and then move the mouse pointer down along the left edge of the screen. What is your result?

A. The Start screen closes and the desktop displays.

B. The Weather app opens and fills the screen.

C. All the open apps display as thumbnail images.

9 Which of the following best describes the group of apps that display as open?

A. Weather, Desktop

B. Maps, Store, Weather

C. Weather, Maps, Store, Desktop

10 On the left side of the screen, point to each open app, right-click, and then click **Close** so that all apps are closed. What is your result?

A. The desktop redisplays.

B. The search results for *store* redisplay.

C. The Start screen displays.

To complete this project: Display the **desktop**, on the taskbar click the **Word** button, and type your answers into the correct boxes. Save and close your Word document, and submit as directed by your instructor. **Close** ☒ all open windows.

END | You have completed Project 1C

CHAPTER REVIEW

PROJECT FILES

For Project 1D, you will need the following files:

Your USB flash drive containing the student data files

Win81_1D_Answer_Sheet (Word document)

You will save your file as:

Lastname_Firstname_1D_Answer_Sheet

1 Display the **Start screen**; point to the upper left corner and drag down slightly to display any open apps; close any open apps. Display the **desktop**. **Close** ❌ any open desktop windows. On the taskbar, click **File Explorer**. In the **navigation pane**, click your **USB drive** that contains the student files for this chapter, and then navigate to **Chapter_Files ▶ Chapter_01**. Double-click the Word file **win81_1D_Answer_Sheet** to open Word and display the document. If necessary, at the top click Enable editing; be sure the window is maximized. In the upper left corner, click **FILE**, click **Save As**, click **Computer**, and then click **Browse** to display the **Save As** dialog box. In the **navigation pane**, click your **USB drive** and then double-click to open your **Windows 8.1 Projects** folder. Using your own name, save the document as **Lastname_Firstname_1D_Answer_Sheet** Click **Save**.

On the taskbar, click the **Word** button to minimize the window and leave your Word document accessible from the taskbar. **Close** the **Chapter_01** window. As you complete each step in this project, write the letter of your answer on a piece of paper; you will fill in your Answer Sheet after you complete all the steps in this project.

Open **File Explorer**, navigate to your **USB flash drive**, and then click to select the **Bell_Orchid** folder. On the ribbon, on the **Home tab**, in the **Clipboard group**, click **Copy**. To the left of the **address bar**, click the **Up** button one time, and then double-click your **Documents** folder to open it. On the **Home tab**, click **Paste**. *You will need a new copy of the files for this Project.* If a message indicates **Replace or Skip Files**, click **Replace the files in the destination** so that you have a new copy of the original files from your USB drive.

From the **navigation pane**, if necessary expand **This PC**, and then double-click your **Documents** folder to open its window. Locate and then double-click the **Bell_Orchid** folder. In the **file list**, how many *folders* display?

A. Four

B. Five

C. Six

2 Navigate to **Bell_Orchid ▶ Corporate ▶ Food_Beverage**. If necessary, change the view to Details. How many *folders* are in the **Food_Beverage** folder?

A. Three

B. Two

C. One

(Project 1D Working with Windows, Programs, and Files continues on the next page)

3 Open the **Restaurants** folder, and then click one time to select the file **Breakfast_Continental**. On the ribbon, click the **Home tab**. In which group of commands can you change the name of this file?

A. New

B. Select

C. Organize

4 With the **Breakfast_Continental** file still selected, point to the file name and right-click. Which of the following is *not* true?

A. From this menu, you can rename the file.

B. From this menu, you can print the file.

C. From this menu, you can move the folder to another folder within Bell_Orchid.

5 Click on the desktop to close the shortcut menu, and then click the **Up** button to move up one level in the hierarchy and display the file list for the **Food_Beverage** folder. On the ribbon, click the **View tab**. In the **Layout group**, click **Large icons**. What is your result?

A. The window fills the entire screen.

B. Files that are pictures are visible as pictures.

C. Only picture files display in the file list.

6 On the **View tab**, return the **Layout** to **Details view**. In the **file list**, click one time to select the file **CO_FB_Menu_Presentation**. In the **Panes group**, click the **Details pane** button. (*Hint*: you can point to a button to see its ScreenTip.) By looking at the displayed details about this file on the right, which of the following is an information item you can determine about this file?

A. The number of words on each slide.

B. The size of the PowerPoint file.

C. The number of people who edited this presentation.

7 In the **Panes group**, click the **Preview pane**. In the **Preview pane**, *slowly* drag the scroll box to the bottom of the scroll bar. Which of the following is *not* true?

A. The slide name displays as you drag the scroll box.

B. The PowerPoint program opens as you drag the scroll box.

C. The slide number displays as you drag the scroll box.

8 In the **Panes group**, click the **Preview pane** button again to close the pane. **Close** ☒ the window. Display the **Start screen**, type **paint** and then press ⌷Enter⌷ to display the **Paint** program on your desktop. On the taskbar, point to the **Paint** button and right-click. Which of the following is *not* true?

A. From the displayed menu, you can pin this program to the taskbar.

B. From the displayed menu, you can pin this program to the Start screen.

C. From the displayed menu, you can close the Paint program.

(Project 1D Working with Windows, Programs, and Files continues on the next page)

CHAPTER REVIEW

9 Click **Close window**, and then display the **Start screen**. Type **paint** and then in the search results, right-click the name of the **Paint** program to display a menu. Click **Pin to Start** and then click outside the search pane to close it. Point to the bottom of the Start screen to display the scroll bar, and then scroll to the right. Which of the following is true?

A. Windows 8.1 creates a tile for the Paint program on the Start screen.

B. The Paint program opens on your desktop.

C. A tile for the Paint program flashes on the Start screen.

10 On the Start screen, point to the **Paint** tile, and then right-click. On the displayed menu, click **Unpin from Start**. Click the **Desktop** tile. Open **File Explorer**, display your **Documents** folder, and then click the **Bell_Orchid** folder one time to select it. On the **Home tab**, in the **Organize group**, locate **Delete**, and then click the lower portion of the button—the **Delete button arrow**. What is your result?

A. The window for the Recycle Bin displays.

B. The folder is deleted and the Documents window closes.

C. A list of Delete options displays.

On the list, click **Permanently delete** (or Recycle if you prefer). Recall that you still have the original Bell_Orchid file on your USB flash drive. In the **Delete Folder** dialog box, click **Yes**. In the upper right corner of the window, click **Close** ☒.

To complete this project: On the taskbar, click the **Word** button, and then type your answers into the correct boxes. Save and close your Word document, and submit as directed by your instructor. **Close** ☒ all open windows.

> **END |You have completed Project 1D**

CONTENT-BASED ASSESSMENTS

Mastering Project 1E Windows Help and Support

In the following Mastering Windows 8.1 project, you will capture and save a snip that will look similar to Figure 1.59.

Apply 1A skills from these Objectives:

1 Use File Explorer and Desktop Apps to Create a New Folder and Save a File on a Removable Storage Device

2 Identify the Functions of the Windows 8.1 Operating System and Windows Store Apps

3 Use Windows Store Apps

4 Sign Out of Windows 8.1 and Turn Off Your Computer

5 Manage User Accounts

PROJECT FILES

For Project 1E, you will need the following file:

New Snip file

You will save your file as:

Lastname_Firstname_1E_Close_App_Snip

PROJECT RESULTS

FIGURE 1.59

(Project 1E Windows Help and Support continues on the next page)

CONTENT-BASED ASSESSMENTS

1 On the **Start screen**, type **help and support** and press Enter to display the **Windows Help and Support** window. Search for **close an app** Click **How do I close an app? Maximize** ◻ the window.

2 On the taskbar, click **Snipping Tool**, click the **New button arrow**, and then click **Window Snip**. Click anywhere in the **Windows Help and Support** window to capture it.

3 On the toolbar of the **Snipping Tool** mark-up window, click the **Highlighter** and then highlight the text *How do I close an app?* Click the **Save Snip** button.

4 In the displayed **Save As** dialog box, in the navigation pane, scroll down, and then under **This PC**, click your USB flash drive. In the **file list**, open your **Windows 8.1 Projects** folder so that its name displays in the address bar, and then as the **File name**, and using your own name, save the snip as **Lastname_Firstname_1E_Close_App_Snip**

5 Close ⊠ the **Snipping Tool** window. Take a moment to click the circled play button to watch the short video about how to close an app.

6 Close ⊠ the Windows **Help and Support** window. Submit your snip file as directed by your instructor.

END | You have completed Project 1E

CONTENT-BASED ASSESSMENTS

Apply 1B skills from these Objectives:

6 Use File Explorer to Display Locations, Folders, and Files

7 Start Programs and Open Data Files

8 Personalize Your Windows 8.1 Start Screen

9 Create, Rename, and Copy Files and Folders

10 Move and Delete Files and Folders

In the following Mastering Windows 8.1 project, you will capture and save a snip that will look similar to Figure 1.60.

PROJECT FILES

For Project 1F, you will need the following file:

New Snip file

You will save your file as:

Lastname_Firstname_1F_San_Diego_Snip

PROJECT RESULTS

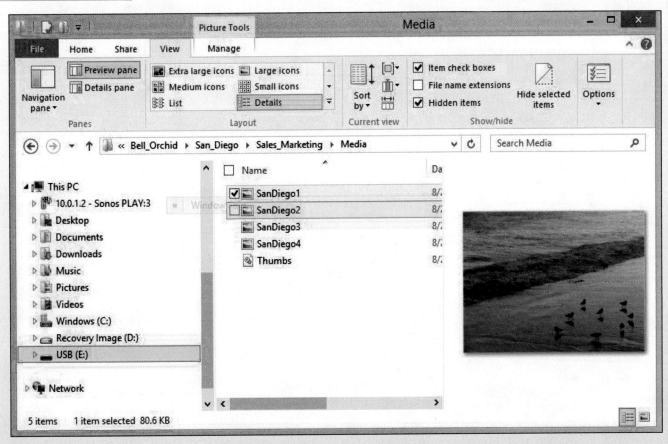

FIGURE 1.60

(Project 1F Working with Windows, Programs, and Files continues on the next page)

END OF CHAPTER

1 Display the **desktop**, and then on the taskbar, click **File Explorer**. Display the window for your **USB flash drive**, and then navigate to **Bell_Orchid ▶ San_Diego ▶ Sales_ Marketing ▶ Media**.

2 On the **file list**, click one time to select the file **SanDiego1**.

3 Display the **Preview pane** for this file.

4 Start **Snipping Tool**, create a **Window Snip**, click anywhere in the **Media** window to capture it, and then click the **Save Snip** button.

5 In the displayed **Save As** dialog box, in the **navigation pane**, scroll down, and then under **This PC**, click your **USB flash drive**. In the **file list**, open your **Windows 8.1 Projects** folder so that its name displays in the **address bar**, and then as the **File name**, and using your own name, save the snip as **Lastname_Firstname_1F_San_Diego_Snip**

6 **Close** ☒ the **Snipping Tool** window. Turn off the display of the **Preview pane**. **Close** ☒ the window. Submit your snip file as directed by your instructor.

END | You have completed Project 1F

OUTCOMES-BASED ASSESSMENTS

RUBRIC

The following outcomes-based assessments are *open-ended assessments*. That is, there is no specific correct result; your result will depend on your approach to the information provided. Make *Professional Quality* your goal. Use the following scoring rubric to guide you in *how* to approach the problem, and then to evaluate *how well* your approach solves the problem.

The *criteria*—Software Mastery, Content, Format and Layout, and Process—represent the knowledge and skills you have gained that you can apply to solving the problem. The *levels of performance*—Professional Quality, Approaching Professional Quality, or Needs Quality Improvements—help you and your instructor evaluate your result.

	Your completed project is of Professional Quality if you:	Your completed project is Approaching Professional Quality if you:	Your completed project Needs Quality Improvements if you:
1-Software Mastery	Choose and apply the most appropriate skills, tools, and features and identify efficient methods to solve the problem.	Choose and apply some appropriate skills, tools, and features, but not in the most efficient manner.	Choose inappropriate skills, tools, or features, or are inefficient in solving the problem.
2-Content	Construct a solution that is clear and well organized, contains content that is accurate, appropriate to the audience and purpose, and is complete. Provide a solution that contains no errors in spelling, grammar, or style.	Construct a solution in which some components are unclear, poorly organized, inconsistent, or incomplete. Misjudge the needs of the audience. Have some errors in spelling, grammar, or style, but the errors do not detract from comprehension.	Construct a solution that is unclear, incomplete, or poorly organized; contains some inaccurate or inappropriate content; and contains many errors in spelling, grammar, or style. Do not solve the problem.
3-Format & Layout	Format and arrange all elements to communicate information and ideas, clarify function, illustrate relationships, and indicate relative importance.	Apply appropriate format and layout features to some elements, but not others. Overuse features, causing minor distraction.	Apply format and layout that does not communicate information or ideas clearly. Do not use format and layout features to clarify function, illustrate relationships, or indicate relative importance. Use available features excessively, causing distraction.
4-Process	Use an organized approach that integrates planning, development, self-assessment, revision, and reflection.	Demonstrate an organized approach in some areas, but not others; or, use an insufficient process of organization throughout.	Do not use an organized approach to solve the problem.

OUTCOMES-BASED ASSESSMENTS

GO! Think | Project 1G Help Desk

In this project, you will construct a solution by applying any combination of the skills you practiced from the Objectives in Projects 1A and 1B.

PROJECT FILES

For Project 1G, you will need the following file:

win01_1G_Help_Desk

You will save your document as:

Lastname_Firstname_1G_Help_Desk

From the student files that accompany this chapter, open the **Chapter_Files** folder, and then in the **Chapter_01** folder, locate and open the Word document **win01_1G_Help_Desk**. Save the document in your **Windows 8.1 Projects** folder as **Lastname_Firstname_1G_Help_Desk**

The following email question arrived at the Help Desk from an employee at the Bell Orchid Hotel's corporate office. In the Word document, construct a response based on your knowledge of Windows 8.1. Although an email response is not as formal as a letter, you should still use good grammar, good sentence structure, professional language, and a polite tone. Save your document and submit the response as directed by your instructor.

To: Help Desk

We have a new employee in our department, and as her user picture, she wants to use a picture of her dog. I know that Corporate Policy says it is ok to use an acceptable personal picture on a user account. Can she change the picture herself within her standard user account, or does she need an administrator account to do that?

END | You have completed Project 1G

OUTCOMES-BASED ASSESSMENTS

GO! Think | Project 1H Help Desk

In this project, you will construct a solution by applying any combination of the skills you practiced from the Objectives in Projects 1A and 1B.

PROJECT FILES

For Project 1H, you will need the following file:

win01_1H_Help_Desk

You will save your document as:

Lastname_Firstname_1H_Help_Desk

From the student files that accompany this chapter, open the **Chapter_Files** folder, and then in the **Chapter_01** folder, locate and open **win01_1H_Help_Desk**. Save the document in your **Windows 8.1 Projects** folder as **Lastname_Firstname_1H_Help_Desk**

The following email question arrived at the Help Desk from an employee at the Bell Orchid Hotel's corporate office. In the Word document, construct a response based on your knowledge of Windows 8.1. Although an email response is not as formal as a letter, you should still use good grammar, good sentence structure, professional language, and a polite tone. Save your document and submit the response as directed by your instructor.

To: Help Desk

When I'm done using my computer at the end of the day, should I use the Sleep option or the Shut down option, and what's the difference between the two?

END | You have completed Project 1H

OUTCOMES-BASED ASSESSMENTS

In this project, you will construct a solution by applying any combination of the skills you practiced from the Objectives in Projects 1A and 1B.

For Project 1I, you will need the following file:

win01_1I_Help_Desk

You will save your document as:

Lastname_Firstname_1I_Help_Desk

From the student files that accompany this chapter, open the **Chapter_Files** folder, and then in the **Chapter_01** folder, locate and open **win01_1I_Help_Desk**. Save the document in your **Windows 8.1 Projects** folder as **Lastname_Firstname_1I_Help_Desk**.

The following email question has arrived at the Help Desk from an employee at the Bell Orchid Hotel's corporate office. In the Word document, construct a response based on your knowledge of Windows 8.1. Although an email response is not as formal as a letter, you should still use good grammar, good sentence structure, professional language, and a polite tone. Save your document and submit the response as directed by your instructor.

To: Help Desk

I am not sure about the differences between copying and moving files and folders. When is it best to copy a file or a folder and when is it best to move a file or folder? Can you also describe some techniques that I can use for copying or moving files and folders? Which do you think is the easiest way to copy or move files and folders?

END | You have completed Project 1I

Index

G

GUIs (graphical user interfaces), 18

H

hard disk drives, 10
    copying files from removable storage
        devices, 45–46
hierarchies, definition, 30
Home tab, 39
hotmail.com, 4

I

icons, definition, 8, 18
immersive apps, 17
insertion point, definition, 20
Internet Explorer, 30
    definition, 8

J

JPEG (Joint Photographic Experts
    Group), 16
Jump Lists, 9

K

keyboard shortcuts, definition, 22

L

libraries
    displaying, 32–38
    Documents
        address bar, 34
        Back button, 34
        column headings, 34
        copying files from removable storage
            devices to, 45–46
        File list, 34
        Forward button, 34
        Library Tools contextual tab, 34
        Minimize button, 34
        Navigation pane, 34
        Recent button, 34
        ribbon, 34
        Search box, 34
        Status bar, 34
        Up button, 34
    navigation pane, 11
live.com, 4
live tiles, 7
local accounts, 4
locations, 4, 10
Lock screen, definition, 5
lock screen apps, 5

M

menu bar, definition, 14
menus, definition, 14

Microsoft account, 4, 26
Microsoft Word, 40
Minimize button, Documents library, 34
modern design, 17
mouse pointer, definition, 8
moving
    files, 50–51
        snapping two windows, 52–53
    between Start screen and Desktop,
        23–24
msn.com, 4

N

names
    folders, 46–47
    tabs, 12
navigation, 10
navigation pane, 11
    displaying folder structures, 38–39
    Documents library, 34
    Favorites, desktop shortcuts, 43
    Open dialog box, 41
Navigation tab, 27
Network area, 8
Network notification icon, 8
Notification bar, 31

O

OneDrive, 10
Open dialog box, 40, 41
open-ended assessments, 69
opening files, 39–43
operating systems
    definition, 3
    functions, 17
outcomes-based assessments, 69–72
outlook.com, 4

P

Paint, 39
parent folder, 34
Paste command, 49
paths, definition, 12
PC settings, 26–28
Pen button arrow, 15
personal folders, 46
personalizing Start screen, 44–45
Pinch, 14
PING (Portable Network Graphic), 23
pinning programs to Taskbar, 9
.png files, 23
pointers, definition, 18
pointing devices, definition, 18
Portable Network Graphic (PING), 23
Preview pane, 37–38
Program buttons, 8
programs
    definition, 3
    desktop shortcuts, 43

    pinning to Taskbar, 9
    starting, 39–43
progress bar, 32
properties (file), 37

Q-R

Recent button, Documents library, 34
rectangular snip, definition, 14
Recycle Bin, 8
    deleting items, 53
Red Pen, 15
removable storage devices
    copying files to Documents library, 45–46
    creating folders on, 10–12
renaming folders, 46–47
resources, definition, 18
restoring deleted items, 53
ribbon
    copy to command, 46
    definition, 11
    Documents library, 34
roaming, 5

S

saving files, 13–16
screen captures, definition, 9
screen elements, 3
screenshots
    definition, 9
    Windows Store apps, saving as files,
        23–24
ScreenTips, definition, 32
scroll arrows, definition, 13
scroll bars, definition, 13
scroll boxes, definition, 13
Search box
    Documents library, 34
    Open dialog box, 41
Search charm, 25
searching for apps, 9
selecting, definition, 12
Settings charm, 25
Share charm, 25
SharePoint, 45
shortcut menus, 11
shortcuts, desktop, 43
shutting down computer, 24–26
signing in to user accounts, 5–8
signing out of Windows 8.1, 24–26
skills review assessments, 60–64
Sleep command, 24
Snap feature, copying and moving files,
    52–53
Snipping Tool, 9
snips, 14
    definition, 9
Speakers icon, 8
split buttons, definition, 8, 14
Start charm, 25
starting programs, 39–43